In 1974, the fiftieth anniversary of the publication of *When We Were Very Young*, Christopher Milne published *The Enchanted Places*: a book about his boyhood in Sussex and the experience of being the model for A. A. Milne's Christopher Robin. This was followed by *The Path Through the Trees* in 1979 and *The Hollow on the Hill* in 1982. Of these three books the *Good Book Guide* has written as follows:

'No doubt about it, these books belong with the classics of autobiography – they can be re-read time and again . . .

'*The Enchanted Places*, a book full of glorious detail, gives a unique view of the making of a myth, for the Pooh tales *are* among the century's proved mythic inventions. How did the little Christopher Milne come to terms with his alter ego Christopher Robin? Ah, there's a story there. Don't be deceived by the light touch and engaging manner. The portraits of Father, Mother, of much-loved Nanny and Christopher are penetrating indeed.'

Frontispiece: Christopher Milne

The Enchanted Places □□□ by Christopher Milne

Methuen

First published in 1974
by Eyre Methuen Ltd

Reprinted in 1975, 1977 and 1980
This paperback edition first published in 1983
by Methuen London, Michelin House,
81 Fulham Road, London SW3 6RB
Reprinted in 1991

ISBN 0 413 54540 7

Printed and bound in Great Britain
by Redwood Press Limited, Melksham, Wiltshire

For Olive Brockwell
"Alice" to others
but "Nou" to me.
To remind you of those enchanted places
Where the past will always be present.

Acknowledgements

The author and the publishers wish to thank Mr Andrew Holmes, who made the film *Mr Shepard and Mr Milne* (photographer Bob Davis), for giving them access to his documentary material on E. H. Shepard and A. A. Milne, and for permission to reproduce the photographs in the frontispiece and in plates 4b and 5b; also to Mrs Vera Joel for the photograph in plate 2b.

Thanks for the loan of photographs are also due to Mrs Tatjana Peppe (plate 2a), Mrs Marjorie Murray-Rust (plate 8) and Mrs Olive Brockwell (plates 1a, 1b, 3, 6a and 7); and to E. H. Shepard and Curtis Brown Ltd for the use of drawings by E. H. Shepard at chapter openings, and in plates 4a, 5a and 6b.

Contents

Contents

Illustrations

"*So they went off together. But wherever they go, and whatever happens to them on the way, in that enchanted place on the top of the Forest a little boy and his Bear will always be playing.*"

The House at Pooh Corner

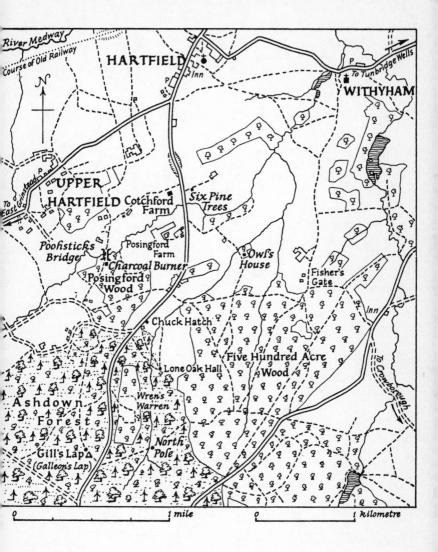

The Enchanted Places

Introduction

From time to time I get a letter from an unknown asking for my help. The sender is a student (or it may be a teacher) and is writing a thesis (or it may be a research paper), and the subject is A. A. Milne (or it may be "Winnie-the-Pooh"). And he (or it may be she) would be grateful if I could oblige by answering a few questions about myself.

Forty years ago such letters were addressed to my father, and I can well remember seeing them on the breakfast table every morning and watching him open them. There were letters from students requesting biographical details; there were letters from children wanting autographs; letters from hopeful imitators asking for advice on how to get their books published; letters from Secretaries of Societies requesting his presence at some function or other; even occasional letters from people down on their luck, short of cash and grateful for anything that could be spared. He would read them silently, then pass them, one at a time, to my mother.

"What do you think?"

"Probably Wol."

"I thought so too."

So "Wol" it often was.

You may remember the occasion. Rabbit had found the notice saying GON OUT BACKSON BISY BACK-SON and had taken it round to Owl for his advice. You may even remember the actual lines. Owl asks:

"What did you do?"

"Nothing."

"The best thing," said Owl wisely.

Somehow, so often, nothing did seem the best thing to do. To answer them was impossible. To explain why you couldn't answer them seemed unnecessarily unkind. So they remained unanswered. "Wol." And now that these letters are coming my way, I, too, find that "Wol" is often the best, indeed the only possible thing. But it leaves me feeling unhappy. . . .

To some extent, then, this book is an attempt to salve my conscience; and it may perhaps be some slight consolation to all those who have written and waited in vain for a reply that this, in a sense therefore, *is* their reply. Belated, I confess, but at least a fairly full one.

You can call it a sort of companion to the Pooh books. In the first chapters I have attempted a picture of Milne family life, the family life that both inspired and was subsequently inspired by the books. In the later chapters I have attempted a picture of my father. If I have imagined an audience it has been a gathering of Pooh's friends and admirers, and I have tried to answer the sort of questions that I imagined friends of Pooh wanting to ask. They would want to know about the real Pooh and the real Forest and whether there really was an Alice. They would want to know something about the real little boy who played with Pooh in the Forest. And finally they would want to know something about the man who turned all these things into stories and verses. They would not be particularly interested to learn what happened afterwards: what happened to the little boy when he grew up.

Yet the little boy did grow up and it is the grown up little

boy who is writing now. And something of what he was by
nature and something of what he became as a result of his
experience will colour his words.

So if I seem ill at ease posing as Christopher Robin this is
because posing as Christopher Robin does today make me feel
ill at ease. And if I seem to write most happily about the
ordinary things that boys do who live in the country it is
because this is the part of my childhood that I look back upon
with the greatest affection. If I had been a different sort of
person I would have felt it all differently and would have
written a different book.

In other words, I am really making a double appearance,
first as the boy I am describing and secondly as the adult
through whose eyes I am seeing him. If it were obvious how
the one became the other then no more need be said; but it is
not obvious and this leads to the question: Should I perhaps not
fill in the gap? My instinct was to answer "No" and to refuse
for two reasons. First, it had nothing to do with the Pooh story
and so was of no concern to my imagined audience. Secondly,
it is one thing to write about a distant and happy period of
one's life but quite another to write about a nearer and very
much less happy period.

In the end, however, persuasion overcame instinct, and I
have added an Epilogue. I say this now to make it clear that the
story I originally set out to tell comes to an end at the end of
Chapter 22. The Epilogue is a different story addressed to a
different audience. It is the story of the effect on someone's life
of an unusual event that occurred when he was a child. You
may imagine, if you like, an Interval between the two, an
Interval during which the audience can get up and stretch their
legs. And if any of them decide at this point to make for the
exit, I shall quite understand.

CHAPTER 1

The Interview

Cotchford Farm on an August morning somewhere around the year 1932. The penstemons, the bergamots, the phloxes, the heleniums, the rudbeckias, the dahlias and even the solitary coreopsis that had seeded itself so cleverly in the paving stones by the sundial had all been told the evening before that today they must look their best. But as yet – for it was barely ten o'clock – there was only one person in the garden to see how nicely they were doing it. He was a tall man, dark and handsome, wearing a brown suit and a brown homburg hat, and he was sweeping the brick path that ran beside the house. For it was Saturday.

George Tasker always swept the path on a Saturday, not because it particularly needed a weekly sweep (though today was different) but because Saturday morning was when he got paid. The shyness and embarrassment that this always caused him had led him to devise a sort of ritual to which my mother had learned to respond. He didn't like to knock on the door. He couldn't just stand around hoping to be noticed. Pulling up weeds from the beds by the house was her work, not his. While if he did anything more distant, he might never get seen at all.

7

So he brought down his big brush and swept; and this made just the right amount of noise, not enough to disturb the Master but enough to remind the Mistress in case she had forgotten.

She had not forgotten. The side door opened and she emerged.

"Good morning, Tasker."
"Good morning, Madam."

A brief conversation followed, for this too was part of the ritual. The Mistress said how pleased she was that it was all looking so pretty today, because someone was coming down from London specially to see it; and Tasker agreed modestly that it was looking quite nice. The Mistress said weren't we lucky with the weather; and Tasker said weren't we, though we could do with a drop of rain. And then the moment arrived and the pound notes were able to change hands and Tasker was able to sound slightly surprised as well as grateful, as if he had forgotten all about its being Saturday. A moment later the Mistress excused herself as she still had rather a lot to do to get everything ready; and Tasker, after sweeping another yard of path to complete the ritual, shouldered his broom and went home.

Let us call her Miss Brown. Miss Brown was a journalist and she was coming down from London to meet us, to be shown around, to ask a lot of questions and then to write an article about us for a magazine. So my mother (after paying Tasker) was going round the garden tidying things away – golf clubs on the putting lawn, a fishing net by the stream, a pullover and a cushion in the Alcove, a copy of last week's *Observer* folded open at the Torquemada crossword in the Garden House – things that my father and I had left lying about. My father was in his room working. And I was already beginning to feel slightly sick at the thought of having to meet someone strange.

I had been told that I must: that she would expect to see me and that it would seem odd if I weren't there, but that I needn't do more than make an appearance, just be around when she arrived and then slide off. Would I have to change? Perhaps a clean shirt and a better pair of trousers and a comb through the hair wouldn't be a bad thing. My father wondered gently which side I usually parted my hair these days; and I remember thinking this odd because I had always parted it on the left.

After lunch we retired to our various bedrooms to make ourselves presentable and to think our various thoughts. My mother's room was large and beautiful. It spanned the full width of the house at its narrow waist. So there was a window in the west wall that looked towards the dovecot and the azaleas (alas, now over) and away to the setting sun; and there was a window in the east wall from which you could see the big lawn, the Garden House and the Six Pine Trees, and through which shone the early morning sun. As she got herself ready she was rehearsing once again the tour that she had planned: the rooms to be hurried by, the rooms where one could linger, the features that the eye could be directed towards, the route round the garden that would show it at its best, the places where one might pause, as if for breath, and wait (hopefully) for admiration. As she rehearsed, so she muttered to herself; as she muttered, so, now and again, she smiled. . . .

My father's room was small and dark, with a window that looked over the courtyard at the kitchen. He was brushing back his thin, fair hair. If Miss Brown liked the house and the garden, and if – which was really the point – she said so loudly and clearly; if she was a genuine Pooh fan and not just someone who muddled you up with A. P. Herbert; if she was young and pretty and gay and laughed in the right places; if all these things, then it might be rather fun. . . .

My room was next door, a large room with a high ceiling that went right up into the roof, and a floor so sloping it was an uphill walk to the window. I was trying not to think about

Miss Brown at all, thinking instead of the things I was going to do when I had slipped away. In imagination I was already wearing again the clothes I had just taken off and was down by the river. It would be a good day for seeing if I could find any new crossing places. . . .

At last we were ready and waiting. Then came the sound of a car lurching in and out of the ruts along our lane followed by the crunch of gravel as it turned into our drive. The Milnes trooped out to welcome their guest.

Nervous laughter. Introductions.

"And this is our boy."

"How do you do, Christopher Robin."

"How do you do."

There. It wasn't too bad. I had looked her bravely in the eyes and smiled my smile. And now we were moving towards the house. My mother led the way, my father and Miss Brown close behind. Gay chatter, in which I was not expected to join. So I tagged along at the back. A cat appeared and I stooped to reassure it, glad of an excuse to drop behind still further.

A hasty glance into my father's room, then into the drawing-room.

"Oh, isn't this wonderful! And you've done it all yourselves! How old did you say it was? Queen Anne? These beams look as if they were once ships' timbers. Oh, what gorgeous flowers. . . ." Miss Brown had been well trained.

Then at last through the French windows and out into the garden, my father and Miss Brown now leading the way. My mother dropped back.

"You can slide off now, Pip, dear, if you like."

So I slid. First up to my room to get back into my comfortable clothes and Wellington boots; then, after a cautious glance through the landing window to see that they weren't still lurking by the house, quickly downstairs and through the front door. I didn't want to be seen. It would look silly to be caught sneaking off like this. By going out through the front door I could keep the house between us, and all would be well. I would have to go rather a long way round: up the lane and then turn down by the duck pond; but I'd be there soon enough.

Five minutes later I had my right boot wedged into an alder stump, right hand clutching a branch, left hand reaching out towards a willow, left boot dangling in space above the brown water. And there I paused to enjoy to the full the wonderful feeling of being alive. . . .

It was evening. Miss Brown had gone and I was back. My mother was in the garden quietly pottering, reliving those glorious moments, hearing again those wonderful, heart-warming words. Miss Brown had noticed everything *and* she had commented. She had specially remarked on the dahlias, Tasker's pride and joy. He must be told on Monday. . . . Gently muttering, gently smiling, my mother moved among her flowers, basking like a cat in the evening sun and in the memory of the praise that had been lavished on her and her beloved garden.

My father was on the putting lawn, pipe in mouth, stooping over his putter, deeply absorbed. One under twos and three to go. It looked as if it might be a record. He, too, still felt a glow from Miss Brown's visit. He, too, loved praise. True there had been a moment when he had found himself wondering if she had ever actually read any of the books. But perhaps it had been a long time ago and she had forgotten. Anyway, she was a dear and very pretty and had said nice things, just as he had hoped. One under twos. He concentrated again on the ball, and as he hit it the sun slipped behind one of the branches of the group of alders on the bridge and a tiny breath of cold air rustled the leaves of the poplar and made a tiny cold echo in his thoughts, so tiny at first that he could scarcely identify it. He watched the golf ball curving down the slope, but he had aimed too high and it was not coming down properly. Could it be jealousy? Today's Milne feeling jealous of the Milne that wrote those books five – ten – years ago? Could one feel jealous of one's self? Or was it something else? Something gone, something lost? She had asked what he was writing now. "A novel," he had said. "Will you ever write another book about Christopher Robin and Pooh, do you think?" Why do they always ask that? Can't they understand? He sighed and walked towards his ball.

I was upstairs in what was known as the Carpenter's Shop, my own private room at the very top of the house, a room whose floor and beams were so eaten away by woodworm that visions of it have haunted my dreams ever since. Yet it was a room I loved, because here I could be alone with my chisels and my saws. Each tool was labelled in my mind with the date and the occasion on which I had acquired it. Many of them had been bought four years before, one by one, out of my weekly pocket money, from the ironmongers in Sloane Square as Nanny and I walked home from Gibbs. Many of them, complete with their labels, were to survive another forty years. I was busy perfecting a burglar alarm that I was planning to fit inside the door of the Secret Passage; and the evening sun, coming in through the window, was shining on my work. It would soon be dinner time. After dinner there would be another chapter or two of Wodehouse, my mother reading, my father and I listening. Then, tomorrow being Sunday, I wouldn't be going riding, so might go exploring instead. How nice it was to feel that there was so much of the holidays still left.

And what of Miss Brown? Can we try and guess her thoughts.

She was in her car speeding back to London, in her handbag her notes, in her head her memories. She too was glowing. It had been an unforgettable day. She had been anxious and nervous, but it had all gone perfectly. She felt stimulated and pleased with herself, and she was already beginning to put together sentences to describe it, making a collection of appropriate adjectives: old-world, mellow, golden, peaceful. Her delight with the house and garden had been quite genuine. You could see how this setting had inspired the books – though it was an odd little room that Mr. Milne had chosen as his study. You would have thought a ligher, sunnier room with a view of the garden would have been better. But perhaps it might have been a distraction.

She thought about her notes. Had she got answers to all the questions she had planned to ask? More or less. The main point was that Mr. Milne took his writing very seriously, "even though I was taking it into the nursery," as he put it. There was no question of tossing off something that was good enough for the kiddies. He was writing first to please and satisfy himself. After that he wanted to please his wife. He depended utterly upon doing this. Without her encouragement, her delight and her laughter he couldn't have gone on. With it who cared what the critics wrote or how few copies Methuens sold? Then he hoped to please his boy. This came third, not first, as so many people supposed. Did Christopher Robin or Mrs. Milne help him with ideas? Yes and no, it seemed. There was the Forest and the Five Hundred Acre Wood. These were real. Then there were the animals. They were real, too (except for Owl and Rabbit that he had invented). His wife and his boy (always his boy, never Christopher. Odd!) had, as it were, breathed life into them, given them their characters. What he had done was to write stories round them. The stories were entirely his own invention.

His books seemed to show a great understanding and love of children. Was he very fond of children? Silence. Then: "I am not inordinately fond of them, if that is what you mean, and I have certainly never felt in the least sentimental about them – or no more sentimental than one becomes for a moment over a puppy or a kitten. In as far as I understand them, this under-standing is based on observation, on imagination and on memories of my own childhood."

Another question she had put. "What does your son think about it all now?" (She had given up referring to him as Christopher Robin: nobody else seemed to.) "How has it affected him, being, you might almost say, a household name?" Mr. Milne had answered this question rather more slowly, rather more thoughtfully, perhaps rather less confidently. He hoped it had done him no harm, might even have done some good. His boy seemed perfectly happy and was certainly doing very well indeed at school and enjoying it all. He didn't think he would ever grow up to wish his name was Charles Robert.

Then she had asked what he hoped his son was going to be when he was a man. Mr. Milne had smiled at this. "At present his great interests are mathematics and cricket." "Does he show any inclination to take after you?" "He *is* taking after me. I was a mathematician and a cricketer when I was his age!" "I mean as a writer?" Laughter. Then: "I don't know that I would specially want him to."

Now for some general impressions. Mr. Milne. An odd mixture of opposites: shy, yet at the same time self-confident; modest, yet proud of what he had done; quiet, yet a good talker; warm, yet with a thin lip and an ice cold eye that might, if you said the wrong thing, be pretty chilling; sympathetic, yet unsympathetic to what he felt was stupidity; friendly, yet picking his friends with care. Next, Mrs. Milne. A certain hot and cold about her, too. You had to say the right thing. Obviously very proud of her husband and wrapped up in his work, though perhaps even more wrapped up in her garden. Lastly, Christopher. Didn't really get much of a chance to see him. Only managed a how-do-you-do and then he was gone. Clearly very shy indeed, painfully so. Probably his parents try to keep him out of the limelight, because, whatever his father says, it can't be too easy growing up with all this publicity. "Christopher Robin is saying his prayers." It can't be too pleasant to have that hanging round your neck when you are at school, however good you are at sums. Boys, after all, can be pretty beastly to each other when they try. There must be moments when he does wish his name was Charles Robert and he could be himself. And that long hair, too. Whose idea was that? His mother's or his father's? And when was it finally cut off? That was a question she never dared ask!

Some more thoughts. (The drive back to London would take an hour and a quarter, leaving plenty of time for thinking.) There were the books, four of them. You could read them and enjoy them. Behind them were the Milnes, three of them. You could meet them as she had, and talk to them and see something of the reality that lay behind the books. And somehow that gave the books an added pleasure. Galleons Lap is Gills Lap, a real place, and she'd actually stood there and looked across the Forest to the distant rim of the world. The bridge where they had played Pooh-sticks was a real bridge, looking just like the drawing in the book. Yet that was not all. For behind what she had seen and and been shown lay who-knew-what that she had not been shown. She had seen the drawingroom, but no one had opened for her that door half way down the passage. She had glanced into Mr. Milne's study, but – well, naturally, of course – she had not been allowed to poke about among his papers. Yet what a gold mine lay there. The letters, the half-finished manuscripts, the jottings, even the scribblings on his blotting paper. What a gold mine for somebody, some day . . . perhaps. She had only seen what she had been allowed to see, a show arranged by the Milnes for her especial benefit. But what went on behind the scenes? What, for example, were they doing and saying right now?

But supposing she knew, supposing she were allowed to open every door and poke into every cupboard, supposing she could eavesdrop every conversation, even listen to their silent thoughts. True, this might throw a new light on the books, lead to a deeper understanding of how they came to be written and of their inner significance. But would her search end there? The child is father to the man (as who-was-it said?) And the mother and father and attendant circumstances make the child. One would have to dig back, into Mr. Milne's childhood, meet his family, and then their family, and theirs. One would have to go right back to the beginning of the world to understand it all. And if one did, then what? One would understand, but would the books be any more enjoyable in consequence? Shakespeare was a great poet. Does it lessen our enjoyment of his plays that we know so little about his life, his parents? And anyway, fascinating though it is to see how every effect has its cause, fascinating though it is to track back along the endless chain of effect and cause, is one man's life chain all that more interesting than another's? Is a famous author's necessarily more interesting than that of an unfamous stockbroker?

With these thoughts spinning around in her head, Miss Brown reached Streatham Common. It was now dark. There was more traffic on the road. If she were to get her story back to her office intact, she would have to pay more attention to her driving. . . .

CHAPTER 2
Names

"We had intended to call it Rosemary" (wrote my father[1]), "but decided later that Billy would be more suitable. However, as you can't be christened William – at least we didn't see why anybody should – we had to think of two other names. . . . One of us thought of Robin, the other of Christopher; names wasted on him who called himself Billy Moon as soon as he could talk and has been Moon to his family and friends ever since. I mention this because it explains why the publicity which came to be attached to 'Christopher Robin' never seemed to affect us personally, but to concern either a character in a book or a horse which we hoped at one time would win the Derby."

I have suffered – if not all my life, then at least for the first thirty years of it – from an embarrassment of names. Let me now, with as much clinical detachment as I can manage, look in turn at each of the four mentioned above, together with their more common variants.

[1] In his autobiography *It's Too Late Now*, published in 1939.

BILLY Survived to get itself into my copy of *When We Were Very Young*, which my father inscribed "Billy's own book", but died between there and *Winnie the Pooh*. It did, however, linger on among those friends of the family who knew me in the early 1920s and so made occasional reappearances. But today it is totally extinct.

MOON This was my early attempt at saying "Milne". Superseded Billy within the family around 1925, and thereafter remained my father's only name for me; used by him among his friends and acquaintances on every occasion when something more precise than "my boy" was required. Universally used among close friends and family, my mother only excepted, until after the war. Still surviving here and there.

BILLY-MOON A rare variant of Billy. Now quite obsolete.

CHRISTOPHER ROBIN My official christian names and so still appearing on occasional legal documents, but now generally superseded by "Christopher" even when "christian names in full" are required. My formal name with acquaintances until about 1928, after which determined efforts were made by the family to kill it off. Today used only by complete strangers, some of whom think (or are charitably assumed to have thought) that Robin is my surname.

CHRISTOPHER Used by school friends and the like from about 1929. Used by my mother when introducing me to her friends from about 1938. Now used almost universally. The only name I feel to be really mine.

CHRIS A variant of the above used in the army and today only surviving at Christmastime on two or three Christmas cards.

C.R. An acceptable variant of Christopher Robin, though not widely used.

ROBIN Used only by the Hartfield Platoon of the Home Guard.

CHAPTER 3
Nursery Days

Billy made his appearance at 11,[1] Mallord Street, Chelsea, at 8 o'clock on the morning of August 21st in the year 1920. He had been a long time coming and this may partly explain why he never had any brothers or sisters. It is reported that Mrs. Penn, the cook, on seeing him, went downstairs to inform the Master that he was "tall, like Mistress" – an early promise that was to remain unfulfilled for another sixteen years. What Gertrude said was not recorded.

Gertrude and Mrs. Penn: they really have no more than walking-on parts in this story. But they must be introduced if only to give today's reader the flavour of a middle-class household in the 1920s. Mrs. Penn is a hazy figure, for she left when I was about seven. I see her as small (so she must indeed have been small), round, grey and elderly. Gertrude was small too, but thinner. My mother's family were well-to-do and had dozens of servants from butlers downwards, and among them was Gertrude, my mother's personal maid; and when Miss Dorothy married she was allowed to take Gertrude with her as part of the marriage settlement.

[1] Later renumbered 13.

Domestic staff wore uniform. I imagine that in those days there was a department in Harrods that catered especially for their needs, and thither their mistresses would repair, armed with sets of measurements to be shown the latest uniforms. "This style, if I may say so, Madam, is greatly favoured by the nobility." How little my mother would be influenced by the preferences of the nobility. How much more likely to choose something to match the curtains. Mrs. Penn I see in grey with a very large white apron; Gertrude was in bottle green with a small and elegant apron and a big black bow which she wore in the back of her hair. Mrs. Penn cooked, and seldom left the kitchen except to go up to her bedroom, which she shared with Gertrude on the top floor. Gertrude did everything else. She cleaned the house before breakfast. She laid the fire in the drawingroom. She served at meals. She made the beds. She polished the silver. She went round the house pulling the curtains when it got dark. And when it grew chilly she would apply the match that lit the fire – though to be fair this was something that my mother often managed on her own. And all this she did with quiet efficiency and great solemnity. I never once heard her laugh.

And what about me? Who was there to change my nappies and powder my bottom?

One can never be sure whether a very early memory is a real memory or just the recollection of something which you were told happened. My first memory – if indeed that was what it was – is of lying on a rug in the nursery. There was a screen round me. I looked up and there above the screen was a round kindly face smiling down at me. So I smiled back at it. I was eighteen months old at the time. There had obviously been nannies before that, but either I hadn't taken to them or they hadn't taken to me. This was the one I had been waiting for.

In the domestic hierarchy nannies come somewhere in the middle. There were times when they would join the servants in the servants' quarters and times when they would join the gentry. But mostly their place was with their charge and that was in the nursery. They, too, wore uniforms. There were black-and-white nannies, grey nannies, blue nannies and pink nannies. There were nannies with hats and nannies with veils. My nanny was grey and she wore a veil when out in the street and a white cap and starched cuffs when indoors. We lived together in a large nursery on the top floor. We lived there, played there, ate there – the food being brought up from the kitchen on a tray – and then at the end of the day we retired, each at our appointed time, to the night nursery next door. So much were we together that Nanny became almost a part of me. Consequently it was my occasional encounters with my parents that stand out as the events of the day.

Our first meeting would be after breakfast when I was allowed to visit the dining-room. There was a large chest by the window and this was opened for me and I climbed inside while my father finished his marmalade and my mother ate her apple. Our next meeting was in the drawing-room after tea. In the drawing-room I could play on the sofa or on my father's arm chair. One day, climbing about on the back of his chair I fell off. In exciting books people often give – as they never seem to do in real life – a "whistle of surprise". That's what I gave when I reached the carpet. And for weeks afterwards if I wanted to whistle I had to climb on to my father's chair and fall off. Later I found a simpler way. My final excursion was to the dining-room in the evening. Here, on the floor under the table in the dark, I would play "boofy games" with my mother, getting more and more excited until the arrival of Nanny would bring it all to an end and I would be swept upstairs to my bath.

I enjoyed playing with my mother. This was something she was good at. There were plenty of things she couldn't do, had never been taught to do, didn't need to do because there was someone to do them for her, and she certainly couldn't have coped alone with a tiny child. But provided Nanny was at hand in case of difficulty, she was very happy to spend an occasional half hour with me, playing on the floor, sitting me on her lap to show me how the gentleman rides, reciting (for the hundredth time) Edward Lear's "Calico Pie".

My nursery was in the front of the house facing the street. If I stood on the ottoman where I kept my toys I could look through the bars of the window and see the whole length of Mallord Street below me. It was a quiet, almost deserted street, no cars, no people, no noise, nothing to look at. But if something of importance came, it would announce its arrival and then I could run to the ottoman and climb up and hold on to the bars and watch. If there was a yodelling shout that would be the log man leading a horse that pulled a cart loaded with logs. If there was the ringing of a hand bell, that would be the muffin man with a tray of muffins on his head. If there was a roaring, rattling noise, that would be the coalman pouring sacks of coal through the little holes in the pavement that went down into the cellars. I even got to know the various clicks and creaks that announced the arrival of the organ grinder and so I would be all ready for "Tipperary" when it came. Organ grinders always made me feel sad, and I used to throw them a penny. But the harp man made me feel sadder. He came on Friday evening and set up his stool just opposite my window. I never knew one organ grinder from another, but the harp man was my friend. He had black hair, a small moustache, a dark grey coat and an air of quiet melancholy. I was allowed to go downstairs and cross the road; and I would put two pennies into his little velvet bag.

But of all the noises the most welcome was "Cooooooo-eeeeee". And that was Anne.

Anne Darlington lived half a mile away in a flat in Beaufort Mansions. She was eight months older than I was, and, like me, without brothers or sisters. So instead we had each other and we were as close and inseparable as it is possible for two children to be who live half a mile apart. It was a closeness that extended to my parents, for Anne was and remained to her death the Rosemary that I wasn't.

Anne had a Nanny who wore black-rimmed glasses and a black straw hat. When we were feeling wicked we called her Jam Puff because she had so many chins, and she would pretend not to have heard. Anne also had a monkey whose name was Jumbo, as dear to her as Pooh was to me. When we were six we left Jumbo and Pooh behind and went to Miss Walters' school in Tite Street, and one morning Anne, who always knew things before I did, told me there was no such person as Father Christmas. We sat next to each other in class while Miss Walters did her best to teach us this and that and mostly we got it wrong.

"Christopher Robin, I'm afraid six from nine does not make five."
"No Miss Walters. I'm not very good at easy sums. I'm better at them when they are harder."

I was better, too, at being Andrew Aguecheek and saying that Nay by my troth I knew not but I knew to be up late was to be up late. I was better at singing.

> On the grassy banks
> Lambkins at their pranks
> Woolly sisters, woolly brothers
> Jumping off their feet,
> While their wooooo-leeeee mothers
> Watch by them and bleat.

After three years of this sort of thing I went to Gibbs and learned Latin while Anne moved upstairs into Miss Hunt's class. But we continued to meet in the holidays. At Easter she came and stayed with us at Cotchford, and sometimes again in early summer.

> Where is Anne?
> Head above the buttercups,

Walking by the stream,
Down among the buttercups.

Those were the Buttercup Days, and there, in Shepard's picture, is Cotchford Farm. In late summer I used to join her (alone, while my Nanny was on holiday) at St. Nicholas on the Kent coast. And finally we spent Christmas together at Mallord Street. She and I inevitably drifted apart as we grew older but she and my parents remained devoted to each other, and until I was twenty-five my mother cherished fond hopes that one day we would marry.

"Cooo-eeeee." I ran to the ottoman, climbed up, leaned over the bars and waved; and Anne and her Nanny waved back. Where were we going? To the Albert Memorial in Kensington Gardens? To the Embankment Gardens by the river? Or across the Albert Bridge to Battersea Park? Were we taking our hoops or our skipping ropes?

When Anne and I go out a walk,
We hold each other's hand and talk
Of all the things we mean to do
When Anne and I are forty-two.

But the Christopher Robin who appears in so many of the poems is not always me. For this was where my name, so totally useless to me personally, came into its own: it was a wonderful name for writing poetry round. So sometimes my father is using it to describe something I did, and sometimes he is borrowing it to describe something he did as a child, and sometimes he is using it to describe something that any child might have done. "At the Zoo", for example, is about me. "The Engineer" is not. "Lines and Squares" and "Hoppity" are games that every small child must have played. "Buckingham Palace" is half and half. Nanny and I certainly used to go and watch the changing of the guard, but I must – for a reason that will appear later – disown the conversation. On the whole it doesn't greatly matter which of the two of us did what: I'm happy to accept responsibility. But I must make two exceptions. The first is "In the Dark".

There was one great difference between my father and myself when we were children. He had an elder brother; I had not. So he was never alone in the dark. Lying in bed with the lights out he could so easily be "talking to a dragon" and feeling brave, knowing that if the dragon suddenly turned fierce he had only to reach out a hand and there would be Ken in the next bed. But I could take no such risks. I had to keep reminding myself that the dragon was only a bedtime story one, not a real one. I had to keep reassuring myself that all was safe by staring at the little orange strip of light that ran along the bottom of the night nursery door, by straining my ears to hear the gentle but, oh, so comforting movements of Nanny in the next room. Sometimes she would call out. "I'm just going downstairs. I shan't be a minute.": and then I would wait anxiously for the sound of her returning footsteps. Once I waited and waited until I could wait no more. Something awful must have happened. I got out of bed, opened the night nursery door, crossed the deserted nursery to the door at the far end. And there was Nanny coming upstairs. "You naughty boy. What are you doing?" "O Nanny, you were such a long time; I didn't know what had happened to you." She was cross, but only a little bit, and I didn't mind. It was so lovely to have her back.

I continued to have night fears for a long time. When, later, I went to boarding school, this was my one consolation when the holidays came to an end: there were no dragons in dormitories.

Once – I can't put a date to it, but I think I must have been about ten – my father, when he came to say goodnight to me, asked me an odd question. "Which side do you usually go to sleep on?" he said. I thought for a bit. I didn't really know. So I made a guess. "My right, I think." He nodded. "That's supposed to be the best side," he said. "You're supposed to be more likely to have bad dreams if you sleep on your left, because then you're lying on your heart." Bad dreams! BAD DREAMS! I did have bad dreams, awful dreams about witches. Now I knew why. I had been going to sleep on my left side. . . . In those days I used to lie on my tummy with one hand tucked under the mattress and the other under the pillow. I would start facing one way. After a while I would feel restless and turn over to face the other way. Then over again, and so on until finally I was asleep. So I might end up on my right side, or I might equally well end up on my left. *I must never end up on my left side again!* Whenever I turned on to my left I must keep my eyes open, wide open, staring, however much I longed to shut them. Then I must turn back on to the other side as soon as ever I could. And every night from then on this became the way I had to go to sleep. For how long? For years, I believe.

> I'm lying on my left side . . .
> I'm lying on my right . . .
> I'll play a lot tomorrow
> I'll think a lot tomorrow
> I'll laugh a lot tomorrow . . .
> Good-night!

Before I come to the second poem that I must disown – and the reader may start guessing which one it will be – I must quote from something my father wrote in a "Preface to Parents" for a special edition of the verses and which he later reprinted in his autobiography.

In real life very young children have an artless beauty, an innocent grace, an unstudied abandon of movement, which, taken together, make an appeal to our emotions similar in kind to that made by any other young and artless creatures: kittens, puppies, lambs: but greater in degree, for the reason that the beauty of childhood seems in some way to transcend the body. Heaven, that is, does really appear to lie about the child in its infancy, as it does not lie about even the most attractive kitten. But with this outstanding physical quality there is a natural lack of moral quality, which expresses itself, as Nature always insists on expressing herself, in an egotism entirely ruthless. . . . The mother of a little boy of three has disappeared, and is never seen again. The child's reaction to the total loss of his mother is given in these lines

> James James
> Morrison Morrison
> (Commonly known as Jim)
> Told his
> Other relations
> Not to go blaming *him*.

And that is all. It is the truth about a child: children are, indeed, as heartless as that. . . .

Is it? Are they? Was I? I cannot pretend to know for sure how I felt about anything at the age of three. I can only guess that though I might not have missed my mother had she disappeared, and would certainly not have missed my father, I would have missed Nanny – most desolately. A young child's world is a small one and within it things may have odd values. A teddy bear may be worth more than a father. But the egotism with which (I will admit) a child is born, surely very quickly disappears as attachments are made and relationships established. When a child plays with his bear the bear comes alive and there is at once a child-bear relationship which tries to copy the Nanny-child relationship. Then the child gets inside his bear and looks at it the other way round: that's how *bear* feels about it. And at once sympathy is born and egotism has died. A poem in which my father really does express what I feel is the truth about a child is "Market Square", which ends up:

> So I'm sorry for the people who sell fine saucepans,
> I'm sorry for the people who sell fresh mackerel,

> I'm sorry for the people who sell sweet lavender,
> 'Cos they haven't got a rabbit, not anywhere there!

How well I remember this feeling of sympathy – totally mis-placed, of course – yet agonisingly sincere!

Undoubtedly children can be selfish, but so, too, can adults. By accusing the young of heartless egotism are we perhaps subconsciously reassuring ourselves that, selfish though we still may be, there was once a time when we were worse. . . .

This brings me to the second poem I must disown – "Vespers". It is one of my father's best known and one that has brought me over the years more toe-curling, fist-clenching, lip-biting embarrassment than any other. So let me, for the first time in my life, look it clearly in the eyes and see how things stand between us.

The general impression left by "Vespers" – especially with any one who has heard Vera Lynn singing it – is of a rather soppy poem about a good little boy who is saying his prayers. But if one reads it rather more carefully, one will see that it is nothing of the sort. It is a poem about a rather naughty little boy who is *not* saying his prayers. He is merely pretending; and to his and the author's surprise he has managed to fool a great many people. "Vespers", then, is not a sentimental poem at all: it is a mildly cynical one. But even so, nothing to get worked up about. After all, everyone is naughty sometimes.

So you might think. But it is not quite what my father thought. Let us see what he had to say in that "Preface to Parents".

Finally, let me refer to the poem which has been more sentimentalized over than any other in the book: "Vespers". Well, if mothers and aunts and hard-headed reviewers have been sentimental over it, I am glad; for the spectacle in real life of a child of three at its prayers is one over which thousands have been sentimental. It is indeed calculated to bring a lump to the throat. But even so one must tell the truth about the matter. Not "God bless Mummy, because I love her so", but "God bless Mummy, I know that's right"; not "God bless Daddy, because he buys me food and clothes" but "God bless Daddy, I quite forgot"; not even the egotism of "God bless Me, because I'm the most important person in the house", but the super-egotism of feeling so impregnable that the blessing of this mysterious God for Oneself is the very last thing for which it would seem necessary to ask. And since this is the Truth about a Child, let us get all these things into the poem, and the further truth that prayer means nothing to a child of three, whose thoughts are engaged with other, more exciting matters. . . .

"Vespers", it seems, is not just about what a certain little boy did on a certain occasion. It is the Truth (with a capital T) about a Child (with a capital C). And although I knew that this was my father's general feeling, I had entirely forgotten how uncompromisingly he had expressed himself.

It was at this point, while I was collecting my thoughts together, wondering how to go on, that I noticed the quotation from Wordsworth. It comes in the first of the two passages I have quoted:

Heaven lies about us in our infancy

This is a line from Wordsworth's "Intimations of Immortality". At first glance it seemed at home in its context. But on looking closer I saw that this was far from the case. For the line had been given a new and altogether different meaning. Wordsworth had been saying that Heaven appeared *to the child* to lie around him. My father was saying that this was how it seemed to the *onlooker*. So then I read the whole poem. It is, of course, the Truth about a Child as Wordsworth sees it, and it is the complete reverse of my father's view. And at once it awakened an echo in my heart – as it must have awakened many another echo in many another heart.

Those first affections,
Those shadowy recollections,
Which, be they what they may,
Are yet the fountain light of all our day.

In those days of splendour and glory I certainly felt myself
nearer to God – both the God that Nanny was telling me about
who lived up in the sky and the God who painted the buttercups – than I do today. And so, asked to choose between these
two views of childhood, I am bound to say that I'm for Wordsworth. Maybe he is just being sentimental. Maybe the infant
William has fooled the middle-aged poet in the same way that
the kneeling Christopher Robin fooled so many of his readers.
Maybe my cynical father is right. But this is not how I feel
about it.

Today it is fashionable to maintain that at the age of five a
child is too young to be taught about God. The Divine is beyond
his comprehension. One should wait until he is older. Dare I
suggest that the reverse might be true: that the child of five is
not too young; he is already too old.

I don't really want to get too involved either with Poetry or
with Religious Instruction, nor do I want to spend too long on
my infant knees. Furthermore, in a world heavily over-
populated with sociologists, psychologists and research workers
generally, I am reluctant to set up theories backed by nothing
more than memory against the statistics and case histories of the
opposition. However, this I must say. The Christopher Robin
of that wretched poem is indeed me at the age of three. I retain
the most vivid memories of saying my prayers as a child. They
go back a long way, but I cannot date them. I well recall how I
knelt, how Nanny sat, her hands round mine, and what we
said aloud together. Did my thoughts wander? Were they
engaged on other, more exciting things? The answer – and let
me say it loudly and clearly – is NO. Would I agree that prayer
meant nothing to a child of three? If the stress is on the last

word, I must be careful: I may be thinking of a child of four. All I can accurately say is that I can recall no occasion when this was so.

At this point a picture floats uninvited into my mind. Nothing that ever happened, nothing to do with my parents, purely imaginary. Papa and Mama in church. Both kneeling. Mama's mind, disconnected from her ears, hovering around the Sunday lunch. Papa, squinting through his fingers, studying the hats in the pew in front. No, it's not only the three year old whose thoughts wander.

I said earlier that I was going to have things out with "Vespers". Partly, I must confess, I wanted to get my own back. But there was another reason. This seems the appropriate moment to give credit where credit was due.

And of course credit lies with my Nanny.

She had me when I was very young. I was all hers and remained all hers until the age of nine. Other people hovered around the edges, but they meant little. My total loyalty was to her. To the extent that I was a "good little boy", to the extent that my prayers had real meaning for me at a very early age and continued to have meaning for many years afterwards, and to the extent that all this was something acquired rather than inherited, this was Nanny's doing. Was she a brilliant teacher? Not specially. She was just a very good and very loving person; and when that has been said, no more need be added.

It will now be apparent why, earlier, I disowned the conversation in "Buckingham Palace". This poem, too, gets mentioned in the Parents Preface. " 'Do you think the king knows all about me?' Could egotism be more gross?" I'm prepared to let that go, but not the line that follows:

> Sure to, dear, but it's time for tea.

Listen to Alice saying that: the daily routine clearly far more important for her than the child's question. You find the same thing in the poem "Brownie". Here are the last two lines of each verse. The child is speaking:

I think it is a Brownie but I'm not quite certain
(Nanny isn't certain, too)

and

They wriggle off at once because they're all so tickly
(Nanny says they're tickly, too)

What Nanny actually says on both occasions – and you can hear her saying it, not even pausing in her sewing, not even bothering to look up – is "That's right, dear". Undoubtedly, this is the Truth about Some Nannies. But, as I hope I've now made quite clear, NOT MINE.

When I was eight years old an odd little incident occurred. It is not strictly relevant and I only mention it because it remains so vividly in my mind.

I was in bed, trying to go to sleep, but I couldn't, and as I turned from side to side so I got more restless and wretched. I didn't feel ill. It was something else. A very strange feeling. Something – someone – was stopping me from going to sleep, was keeping me awake. But who? And why? I struggled for an answer and gradually one began to dawn on me.

"Nanny!"
"What is it, dear?"
"Can you come?"
She came at once
"What's the matter?"
"I can't get to sleep."
"Are you feeling all right? Have you got a pain?"
"It's not that."
"What is it, then?"
A pause. Then in a hushed voice:
"Nanny, I think I know. . . . It's God. I think He's cross with me."
"I'm sure He's not dear. Whyever should He be?"
"No, Nanny; He is. And I think I know why. It's because of

that Bible we bought for school. He doesn't like me having two Bibles."

"I don't think He would mind that, dear."

"No, Nanny: He does. I know He does. So can we give it away. Who shall we give it to?"

Nanny thought.

"We could give it to Farm Street. I think they might like it. I'm sure they would."

(Farm Street was a girls' school in Birmingham. The children had been writing to me over a number of years and I used to write back. In April I used to send them bunches of primroses.)

"Oh, Nanny, do let's. Can we do it now?"

"Well, dear . . ."

"Please start doing it."

"It's got your name inside . . . It could be *from* you. I could write 'from' in front of your name. Shall I do that?"

"Yes, do do that. Do it now. Please."

So she did. She went next door and wrote and then she came back and showed me and told me that everything was all right now and that if God had been cross with me, now He had forgiven me, and I could go to sleep, and tomorrow we would post off the book.

Immediately the strange feeling left me and I went to sleep. The next morning the incident was all but forgotten. The Bible was never sent. I took it to school as usual. The "from" (in a different handwriting) always looked a bit odd, but I left it there.

A year later I went to boarding school and Nanny departed. Alfred was waiting for her. Indeed he had been waiting for her patiently for many years. Alfred! My rival! "Nanny, don't marry Alfred. Marry me." But in the end she did. And together they bought a bungalow, and they called it "Vespers".

It was a nice gesture to my father. But only Nanny and I knew what the name really meant.

CHAPTER 4
Soldier

I want a soldier
(A soldier with a busby)
I want a soldier to come and play with me . . .

Daddy's going to get one
(He's written to the shopman)
Daddy's going to get one as soon as he can come.

And Daddy did. And it was one of the most exciting moments
in all our lives when the nursery door opened and a giant
Guardsman in full regalia with scarlet tunic and huge, furry
busby strode into the room, marched up to the tiny boy and
saluted. The tiny boy was totally overcome; so much so that I
cannot in the least recall what happened next. I imagine that I
was allowed to hold his busby, even to try it on, to finger his
buttons and epaulettes and all his accoutrements. Did I sit
on his lap or ride on his back? Did he stay for tea? Did I cry
when at last he said goodbye? But of course he would have
promised to return; and he did – many, many times, though
never again in scarlet. But he was always Soldier to me, indeed
to us all. For after that first, wonderful appearance, how could

34

he have been anything else? Other people knew him as Louis Goodrich, an actor. He was, I believe, a casual acquaintance of my father's at the Garrick Club. One day my father had been talking to him and had mentioned my current passion for the military, and Goodrich had said: "How would he like it if I dressed up and came to see him?" And so it was arranged. The day was chosen, the uniform hired, and thus began a long and close friendship between us.

Some people are "good with children", just as others are "good with animals". It isn't just that they like them and enjoy playing with them. There is a mysterious something about them that the child – or animal – is unconsciously and immediately aware of. The animal loses its fear, the child his shyness. The animal lets itself be touched. The child starts scrambling all over you. So it was with Soldier and me.

He came to tea often – nursery tea, of course; for he came to see me, not my parents. He was such a very wonderful and exciting person that Anne was allowed to share him, and the four of us – Nanny, me, Soldier and Anne – had tea together. When tea was over the business of the afternoon began. The table was cleared. Nanny went down to the kitchen and returned bearing bowls and jugs, rolling pins, pastry boards and egg cups, icing sugar and egg white, peppermint essence and cochineal. "I must have an apron," said Soldier, "the largest apron you can find." Nanny went hunting. Then we started: pouring, mixing, stirring, tasting, adding a bit more of this and a bit more of that, tasting again to make sure, trying the other person's, then scooping, flattening, tasting once more to see if it was still all right, rolling, getting it all wrapped round everything, unwrapping it, laughing, saying "Oh, Soldier, you are so funny!", getting more and more wild and excited, then stamping out with the egg cups, squashing up the remainder, tasting just once more, rolling again, stamping again, looking to see how the others were doing. "Oh, Soldier, *look* what you've done!" ... I can see us still, though the picture is dim at the edges. Soldier is there with his voluminous apron and I believe on one occasion a chef's hat; Anne is there, husky with excitement; Nanny is there; and, yes, I think I can see my mother. . . . But however much I strain my eyes I can see no one else.

Some people are good with children. Others are not. It is a gift. You either have it or you don't. My father didn't – not with children, that is. Later on it was different, very different. But I am thinking of nursery days.

It was difficult for him, of course. For there was Nanny always in the way, Nanny who claimed so much of my affection. And on the rare occasions when Nanny was out of the room, there was my mother in her place. On Nanny's day off there was Gertrude looking after me. Where did he fit in? Nowhere special. And now here was Soldier. You could see how my eyes lit up at the very thought of Soldier, at the mere mention of his name. You could see (or you could be told) how he made me laugh, how I adored him. No, my father couldn't compete. Did this make him, I wonder, a little jealous, a little sad? Did he secretly envy those who had the gift? My poor father! All that was left to him were family visits to the London Zoo or family walks through the Sussex woods, and perhaps a few brief minutes of good-night story.

People sometimes say to me today: "How lucky you were to have had such a wonderful father!" imagining that because he wrote about me with such affection and understanding, he must have played with me with equal affection and understanding. Can this really be so totally untrue? Isn't this most surprising?

No, it is not really surprising, not when you understand.

There are two sorts of writer. There is the writer who is basically a reporter and there is the creative writer. The one draws on his experiences, the other on his dreams. My father was a creative writer and so it was precisely because he was *not* able to play with his small son that his longings sought and found satisfaction in another direction. He wrote about him instead.

CHAPTER 5
Self Portrait

Height: Small for his age.
Weight: Underweight. Needs fattening up.

They did their best, of course, but it was really a waste of time, for no amount of eating has ever had any visible effect on me.

When I was a child I was what grown-ups describe as a fussy eater. That is to say I ate what I liked well enough, and as much of it as I could squeeze in; but what I didn't like I divided up into little bits and pushed around the plate and said "Need I, Nanny?" until she relented and I was allowed to leave it. I accepted that this was how it was with food, part pleasure, part penance. It never occurred to me that the penance part was unnecessary. I used to say that if ever I was sent to prison I would at least enjoy the meals, bread and water being what I was specially fond of. And I said this, not sadly, not complainingly, but almost with pride – a criticism of nursery food all the more telling for being quite unintended.

Why were meals so unappetising? We had a good cook. At the time I'm thinking of Mrs. Penn had left us and been replaced by Mrs. Gulliver. I liked Mrs. Gulliver. She was as large and fat and jolly as Gertrude was small and thin and solemn, and she could produce the most wonderful meals, as I later discovered. Why didn't any of them find their way upstairs? Partly the reason was that nursery meals were served before dining-room meals. This meant that if Nanny and I had been allowed to share in the dining-room roast chicken and chocolate soufflé, neither would have been looking its best when it reached my parents. So for us it had to be shepherd's pie and rice pudding. But this still doesn't explain why the rice pudding was quite so white, quite so stiff, quite so unlovely. This remains a mystery. It was not until I went to prep school that I learned what a proper rice pudding was like and developed an absolute passion for it that has lasted to this day; which is not the sort of thing one normally learns at prep school.

So there I was, not eating enough and not nearly fat enough. Something had to be done, and, as I have said, they did their best. They tried strengthening medicine (which Tigger was so fond of). I was fond of it too, but it didn't make me any fatter. So then they tried gymnasium classes run by two Scotsmen called Munroe and Macpherson. On my first day, as we marched round the gym, horrible Mr. Macpherson shouted out: "Christopher Robin, you look like a camel. Hold yourself up, lad." But though I learnt to climb a rope, I still didn't get any fatter. So then they tried boxing classes. I cantered across the floor and struck Mr. Macpherson on the nose, and he pretended it was a fly tickling him and said: "Harder, lad, harder." But though I was very proud of my boxing gloves, my muscles didn't bulge the way they should. So then finally they tried massage. I lay on the ottoman in the nursery while Mrs. Preston powdered me and then thumped and kneaded. But though I loved it I remained resolutely underweight. And I have done so ever since.

Appearance: Girlish.

Well, what can you expect? I had long hair at a time when

boys didn't have long hair. One day Nanny went into the grocer's shop at the top of Oakley Street and left me lying outside in the pram. And while she was there two people came and peered at me and one of them said: "Oh, what a pretty little girl." That is not the sort of thing one forgets in a hurry. I used to wear girlish clothes, too, smocks and things. And in my very earliest dreams I even used to dream I was a girl.

General Behaviour: Very shy and un-self-possessed.

My father used to reassure me that he was shy too, that on the whole shy people were nicest, and that it was far better to be shy than boastful and self-assertive. But all the same I went a little too far the other way. When people asked me simple questions like did I want another piece of cake, I really ought to have known the answer and not turned to the hovering figure at my side and said "Do I, Nanny?"

General Intelligence: Not very bright.

There was a story – I think it was Anne who told me, many years later – that Miss Walters from my kindergarten was so impressed by my dimness that she got herself invited to tea at Mallord Street to see whether I was always like that or only at school. I don't know what her conclusions were. I don't know whether she came a little nearer to believing that I was not just being silly when I had said that I could do the difficult sums but not the easy ones.

General Interests: Good with his hands.

Here at last was something I was all right at. I used to love making things. I sewed things (the Cottleston Pie that Pooh once sang about was an egg cosy I made) and knitted things and made tapestry pictures. I had a Meccano set and made (among other things) a working grandfather clock. Or rather I made the works and a friend, older than I, came to tea one day and helped me with the case, the weights and the pendulum. That night, however, I couldn't get to sleep. I lay awake all restless and unhappy. Finally, I called out:

"Nanny, can you come?"

"What is it, dear?"

"It's the clock. I don't want to keep it. You see I didn't do it all myself. Alec helped me with it. So can you take it to bits, please: just the stand part. Can you start doing it now?"

So she did: one of the odder things that Nannies get called upon to do.

Then there were the things that I took to bits myself. Using a penknife, I once took a dead mouse to bits to see how it worked. But it was hard to tell exactly and really rather disappointing and so I threw it away. I also took the lock on the night nursery door to bits. I discovered how it worked but not how it went together again. So an ironmonger had to be summoned. What! Couldn't my father have mended it? My *father*, did you say? *Mend* something? Even at the age of seven I was already the family's Chief Mender. And mostly I succeeded. Admittedly the lock was a failure, and another failure was when I tried to run my 6 volt electric motor by connecting it up to the electric light switch. Nothing happened. Even now, looking back on the event with greater electrical knowledge, I still can't understand why *nothing* happened.

It will now, I hope, be apparent why I said in an earlier chapter that the poem "The Engineer" was not about me. The poem begins:

> Let it rain
> Who cares
> I've a train
> Upstairs
> With a brake
> Which I make . . .

and it ends up:

> It's a good sort of brake
> But it hasn't worked yet.

I may have been a bit undersize. I may have been a bit underweight. I may have looked like a girl. I may have been shy. I may have been on the dim side. But if I'd had a train (and I didn't have a train) any brake that I'd wanted to make for it – any simple thing like a brake – WOULD HAVE WORKED.

CHAPTER 6

In the Country

In 1925 my father bought Cotchford Farm and we became countrymen, or, to be more accurate, half-countrymen. For we still spent most of our time in London, going down to Cotchford only at week-ends and for the Easter and summer holidays.

Up to then we had paid only occasional visits to the country. There had been visits to my mother's lovely family home of Brooklands on the Hamble, visits from which survive the memories of a rocking horse and – annually reawakened – the colour and scent of azaleas. There had been a holiday at Woolacombe where I had first encountered what I'm told I called "the huge water" and where – if anywhere – I had got "sand between the toes". There had been a famous holiday in Wales where the first poems of *When We Were Very Young* had been written. And finally there had been visits to Decoy, a thatched cottage near Angmering in Sussex. At Decoy there was a lake. On the lake was a swan. And the swan's name was Pooh. There were woods and meadows, too, and I have hazy memories of these; but it is the little close-up things that a child sees most clearly. I remember beans, smooth, with pink and black blotches, holding them, arranging them, looking at

42

them. I remember butterflies, cabbage whites and meadow browns, caught and held in the hand and examined. I remember daisies, wild daisies, not white as they seem to be to grown-ups, but pink; and I have only to pick one now and turn it over and look closely at the pink underside of its petals to see again the daisies of my childhood.

But Cotchford was different from all these. Cotchford was ours, and on an autumn morning in 1925 we climbed into the blue Fiat, my mother and father in the back, Nanny and I sitting next to Burnside in front, and drove down to take possession.

No. I have got it wrong. It was Cotchford that took possession of us.

My mother had been brought up partly in London, partly in the country. She knew what it was to live in a large country house and sit on lawns and wander past flower beds. London, no doubt, attracted her, especially as she grew older, with its gay parties and its pretty clothes, with its opportunity to escape from her wretched brothers and their muddy knees and everlasting sailing-talk. But at Brooklands her deep and abiding love of gardens was born and with it her love of the peace and the solitude that you can find only in the country.

After the first War she and my father had settled down in London, and she was happy there, being gay and smart and meeting exciting people. And no doubt to begin with this was enough. In any case it wasn't long before I turned up; and if I wasn't a full-time job, I was at least a part-time hobby. But it wasn't until we moved to Cotchford that my mother's talents knew that this was the moment for which they had been all this time quietly waiting. With memories of Brooklands to inspire her, with a succession of books by Marion Cran to guide her, and with seed catalogues and plant catalogues to hand in the bathroom for quiet after-breakfast study, she set to work. And as the money began to come in from the books, so, from time to time, Mr. Berrow appeared, with his horn-rimmed glasses, his plus-fours, his bow tie, pencil and paper to sketch out "proposed plans for terrace gardens, orchard and summer house".

My mother in her garden. Trowel in hand planting Darwin tulips by the hundred. Secateurs in hand snipping at roses. Crouched down, weeding, weeding, weeding. Pouring jugs of hot water over the ants. Exhorting Tasker to ever greater efforts. Teaching me the names of the flowers – lovely names like salpiglossis and spiraea Anthony Waterer, difficult names like eschscholtzia which were fun to spell. But mostly I remember her just quietly, happily, brooding over it all, alone in the half dark.

You can love the country in two quite different ways, as a cat loves it and as a dog loves it. My mother was like a cat. She responded to the beauty, the peace and the solitude that it offered. She found this in her garden and she found it too in the countryside beyond. Solitude. She was happiest alone. Once, when she was going for a walk, I asked if I could come with her. "No," she said, "but come and meet me on my way back. I like best being met." And so we spent a lot of time meeting her. She would walk to the village and half an hour later my father and I would set off up the hill and hope that somewhere before we reached the top we would see her coming round the corner. Or it might be the other way round, and she would meet us as we drove home (choosing the pretty way, of course) after spending the morning playing golf. At night, before going to bed, she would walk up to the forest, two miles along the road, until she was level with Gills Lap. On these occasions I sometimes accompanied her. It was different in the dark. You could be with someone and they would be there if you felt you wanted them, and if you didn't you could forget them. Now and again, on our way, a car would come by: blinding lights, a roar and a whoosh of wind that seemed to suck you out into the road in their wake. We clung to each other, standing against the hedge, until they were gone. Then on again. We both loved the country at night, the black shapes of the trees, the tiny spots of light from wayside cottages, the sound of the wind bustling about its invisible business. We scarcely talked, absorbed in our private thoughts.

If my mother was a cat, my father was surely a dog. He was a Londoner, a real Londoner with a deep love of London in his bones. For him the country had always been, not where you lived, but where you went. Where you went on holiday. Where you went to do something – to ride a bicycle, to climb a hill, to look for birds' nests, to play golf. Like a dog, he couldn't just *be* in the country, sitting or strolling aimlessly. It had to be a proper walk, a walk with a purpose, planned beforehand, worked out on the map even. And you couldn't go alone; you had to be with somebody, with me perhaps, or with the whole family, Nanny included. Like a dog, too, he was happiest of all when chasing a ball.

In front of the house a lawn sloped down to a ditch. It was virtually the only lawn that Cotchford possessed when we first arrived, and at once my father claimed it as his own private preserve, and laid it out for clock golf. And as a clock golf course it always remained, the only bit of the garden where my father reigned supreme. The ditch that bounded its lower edge was widened and turned into a moat, known as "the stream". A marshy bit in one corner was dug out to make a rather unpleasant pond. And eventually the russet apple tree in the middle died and was cut down. But otherwise the putting lawn remained unchanged over the years, and round and round it my father went, round and round and round. If I was at home, I joined him. "Just time for a quick record before lunch?" We played together, not against each other: more friendly that way. If I wasn't there, he played alone; and if he did a particularly good round, he would proudly tell me. When I was at school or away during the war, he would tell me in his weekly letter. He didn't tell my mother: she wouldn't have been specially interested, wouldn't even have known what "two under twos" meant. She never played. She hated all games.

So while my mother dug, my father putted. Does this sound like ant and grasshopper? In a way it was. But you can look at it another way. To each his trade. My father was a writer: this was his work. All he wanted from my mother was her encouragement and praise. My mother was a gardener, and praise and encouragement was all she wished for in return, no need also for a hand with the manuring: we had a full-time professional for that.

The stream was included in my father's domains. It had been hoped at one time that it might make an attractive feature with goldfish and water lilies. But all it seemed able to grow were dense mats of brown weed. Brown scum congealed on its stagnant surface, and strange creatures moved in its depths. So my father was allowed to keep it; and he and I shared it. We plunged nets and golf clubs into it, and piles of weed with their attendant black mud were landed on the bank. We stooped to peer closely. And gradually the various inhabitants would work their way up to the surface, flip-flapping if they were fish, wriggling if they were newts, crawling if they were dragonfly larvae. Each was examined before being put back. Sometimes golf balls came up in the catch, their brownness telling us how long they had lain submerged. Once or twice we caught what my father said was a triton, an extra large, black and nobbly newt, slow-moving and looking prehistoric. This was a great excitement. Sometimes a grass snake would slip into the water and take refuge between the stones that lined the bank. Grass snakes were even more exciting, but they were not welcome for they ate the other creatures. And so they were pursued with putters until landed; and since landing a grass snake with a putter is not easy, we hoped it was also not too unsporting. They were then flung into the bullrushes and told not to come back.

So the garden for my father was where you sometimes looked

1a. Christopher and Nanny

1b. Christopher, Pooh
and Nanny

2a. The sitting room at Cotchford Farm

2b Cotchford Farm from the garden

for newts, but mainly where you putted and where you admired my mother's labours. It was also where, after lunch, you sought out a sheltered spot, and, armed with deck chair, cushions, rugs and pullovers, retired there to reverberate gently until tea time.

These were the things you could do alone. But there were other things which needed two of you. There was cricket and there was catch: cricket could be played in the meadow, and catch with a tennis ball up against the wall. So my father was determined that, however much I enjoyed just being in the country, playing happily by myself, doing nothing happily by myself, however cat-like I was, I was jolly well going to spend some of my time enjoying dog games with him.

I was not immediately enthusiastic. On my fifth birthday I had been given a shining suit of armour, and lived in it, almost went to bed in it, was in tears at the prospect of being unstrapped from it. "One day," said my father to his tiny St. George, "you will be thinking of nothing but cricket." I stared at him aghast. My breast plate, my back plate, the wonderful things that protected my arms (even though slightly too long and rather scratchy round the wrist), my helmet with its red plume and the visor that I could pull down when danger threatened: how could I ever abandon these? "Nothing but cricket," I said in amazement. "Not armour?"

But my father was right.

Cotchford was built on a hillside and so almost everything was on a slope. But there was one level bit, a grass path that, starting off between two giant yews, ran through what we called the orchard. Five feet wide, twenty yards long, and absolutely straight, it would serve admirably; and it was here that I first took up my stance, while my father bowled at me with a tennis ball and Nanny stood at deep cover point to retrieve anything that went down the hill towards the dovecot. Years later a proper pitch was made in the meadow beyond the stream and a net was erected. And on summer evenings I changed into my white flannels (my first long trousers), put on pads and gloves, collected bat and ball, and off we went together. I batted, he bowled. And sometimes an off drive, slightly lofted to clear the thick grass, would almost reach the river; but more often a sweep to leg, flying over the net, would land in the swamp by the willows. "Oh, well hit! Quick!" and we would rush to the spot and tramp up and down among the rushes, while horseflies hovered overhead. Cricket was for summer evenings, and afterwards there was a tray with a jug of lemonade waiting in the diningroom. But catch with a tennis ball, like putting, was for the odd five minutes while waiting for Pat to ring the bell for lunch.

At the edge of the brick path where it ran beneath the nursery window were two small holes, something to do with ventilation. In one of these the tennis ball was kept. We stood about five yards back from the house, on the lawn where the big sycamore grew, and we threw against the wall, hard, as if returning a ball from cover point. We threw to each other, back and forth, and as we caught, so we counted. One, two, three, four, five. . . . A high one from me and my father would leap and bring off a brilliant one-hander while the blue handkerchief he kept up his sleeve fluttered to the ground. "Oh, well held, sir!" Six, seven, eight. . . . A wide one from my father and I would make a dramatic dive, but in vain and the ball shot over the flower bed, bounced across the putting lawn and into the stream. I would fish it out with a golf club and we would start again. What was the world's record? Fifty? A hundred? I forget.

Putting, golf, cricket, catch, these were the things we did together – but not until Nanny had left us and I was at boarding school. Up to then I was much like any other child in the country. I took my toys out and played with them in the grass. I played in the hay, I played in the mud, played in the water, played with friends, played with Nanny, played alone, climbed trees, picked primroses in the spring and nuts in the autumn, went exploring, rode a donkey. To begin with the country was very much for playing in. Later, much later, I began to enjoy long solitary walks. Or I would go down to the river and find a quiet place, secluded, hidden beneath the bank and sit there for hours, watching the water as it gently twisted and eddied past me. Then perhaps I might see something: an eel, wriggling its way upstream; a grass snake with just its black head showing above the surface, moving gently from side to side; damsel flies, their wings making a dry whispering sound as they came to investigate me; the plop of a water vole, and if you looked quickly you might see it running underwater along the river bed; a shy moorhen, a noisy mallard, a flashing kingfisher, whistling urgently. But never, though I waited in hope day after day, never the sight of an otter.

So of the three of us, I suppose it could be said that I was the one most totally captivated by Cotchford, for it gave me all the delight it gave my mother and all the delight – the very different delight – it gave my father; and it continued to do this, on and off, for thirty years.

On an August morning in the year 1942 I said goodbye to Cotchford. The penstemons, the bergamots, the phloxes, the heleniums, the rudbeckias, the dahlias and even the solitary coreopsis that had seeded itself so cleverly in the paving stones by the sundial were still looking as lovely as ever. I said goodbye convinced, absolutely, that I would never return.

During the four years that followed I twice tried to while away moments of idleness by writing about the house and the garden, the fields and the river, the woods and the forest that I knew and loved so well – once when I was in Iraq, later when convalescing in Italy. I wrote happily, page after page, then read what I had written and tore it up.

Now, and for very much the same reasons, I am making my third attempt.

CHAPTER 7

Cotchford Farm, 1932: a Conducted Tour

"Come on. Let me show you round the house.

"In here – mind the step: there are odd steps all over the place because we're built on a hill – in here's the dining-room. Nothing very special, but it's just worth going over to the fireplace because if you stand inside you can look up and see the sky. There was another fireplace like this in the drawing-room. We used to burn peat in it – brown slabs like square biscuits – which was nice and rustic but gave us more smoke and draught than heat. So we had it bricked up and now it's so small you can scarcely burn anything bigger than a matchstick. This one in the dining-room we don't use at all.

"Through that door's the kitchen and the servants' quarters where Mrs. Wilson and Pat live. No need to show it to you, so let's go back into the hall again. . . .

"This is just the downstairs lav and in the corner is the pump. We're not on the mains and get all our water from a well. You can see the well house if you look through the window: that little building under the tree. There are usually two or three frogs living in it, and sometimes a grass snake, but the water tastes all right. Edward Tasker – he's our gardener's nephew – comes every morning after breakfast to do the pumping. There's a tank up in the attic – in my carpenter's shop, actually – and when it's full the water comes out of a pipe and you can hear it splashing down outside. . . .

"Now let's go down the passage. Mind the step. This is my room in here. It used to be my nursery ages ago and we still call it that. It's not used for much: just where things get put, my cricket things and so on. Oh, yes, that's a gas-light. We don't have electricity. We make our own gas out at the back of the kitchen from drums of white stuff. There's a gas-light here, one out in the passage, two more in the drawing-room and another at the top of the stairs. Apart from that we use candles, which is nice and countrified.

"On we go. . . . That's my father's room in there. Not worth looking at. Very small and damp and dark, and after he's been in it all morning smoking his pipe the smell is terrific.

"Now mind the step and don't bump your head. Even I can bump my head on this door. My father is always bumping his head all over the place. He has a perpetual lump in the middle of his bald spot. If you listen you can hear him doing it. Bump! 'OUCH! Oh . . . Oh . . . Oh . . .'. This is the drawing-room and this is where all our visitors start studying the beams in a learned way, saying: 'Ships' timbers'. I can't see why they should have been, myself. They were obviously *something* once because of their odd shapes and holes. But I should have thought it much more likely they came out of somebody else's house or an old barn. . . . Note and admire my mother's 'Constance Spry' flower arrangement, by the way – done specially in your honour. And that's Tattoo asleep on the sofa. We have three other cats and she's their mother. She's had hundreds of other kittens but they've mostly been drowned. She's about seven years old although she looks so small. Now let's go upstairs.

"Let's go right through to the far end first and I'll show you the Secret Passage. You have to go through my mother's bedroom to get to it. This is her room. There's a bees' nest in the roof just outside the window. So a lot of bees come in and die on the window-sill and you have to be a bit careful if you walk round with bare feet. Through here is what used to be my father's dressing-room. It's nothing much now. And here's the front door of the Secret Passage. You can ring the bell if you like. Right. In you go. Mind the burglar alarm. The light switch is over there. This is the only room in the house with electricity. No, it's not really old at all; in fact it's one of the newest bits of the house. I think it was put on just before we arrived. It's where we used to put trunks and suitcases and things. I was playing here one day when I discovered the Passage. So then I sort of took possession and the trunks and things got moved somewhere else. This is the actual Passage over in the corner. You can just about squeeze through. But be careful to tread on the joists or you'll be in the kitchen. The lights down here are fitted to a two-way switch so that I can turn them on and off from either end. My bedroom's at the far end – not my *real* bedroom, of course. It's being a sort of space under the roof that makes it this funny triangular shape. But it's quite long: it runs the full width of the house. The walls were wall papered by me, which was quite a business squatting down here doing it by candlelight. And then I made all the various bits of furniture, the arm chair, the sofa and so on. Seen all you want? Let's go, then.

"The bathroom's in here. The water comes out of the hot tap as brown as tea when you first have a bath at the beginning of a weekend. There's supposed to be a lot of iron in our water: I don't know if that's got anything to do with it. If you try swimming in the river you come out looking like a Red Indian. Spare bedroom in here. It doesn't get used much nowadays. We don't often have people to stay. My father's bedroom is in there. And this is my bedroom. The floor's a bit sloping and you tend to roll out of bed until you're used to it. That little door leads to a sort of dressing-room which was once used for washing in. It's quite handy because it's got a window you can climb out of, which can be useful if there are visitors in the house you don't want to meet.

"Then we've got one more lot of stairs, very winding and dark. Would you like to come up. You're almost certain to bump into something or trip over something, so don't say I didn't warn you. Mrs. Wilson's room's in there. Bad luck; but I did warn you. I expect you'll survive. And here's my carpenter's shop where all the Secret Passage furniture gets made.

"There. You've seen it all now. So let's go outside. I think we've just got time to have a quick look at the river before lunch. We can hear the bell from there. Then after lunch we can do a proper explore and I can show you some of my crossing places and the trees I climb and the marsh where I found the snipe's nest and the weir and Posingford Wood where the charcoal burner used to live. . . . Come on."

CHAPTER 8

Field and Forest

You must start with a map.[1] We kept ours in the drawing-room on the bookshelf by the window. You must start with a map because Cotchford Farm is on the map and this was something we were all very proud of. Look. *Here!* And what is more it is underlined. I used to think that it was the printer who had underlined it, but I realize now it was more likely to have been my mother or my father. And over the years, as countless proud fingers pointed it out to countless admiring visitors, so a sort of grey haze descended upon it, making it even easier to find. But as your map may be a new one, I had better help you.

The map you need is the 1 inch Ordnance Survey Sheet 183.[2] Just off it up in the top left hand corner is East Grinstead, and just off it up in the top centre is Tunbridge Wells. The village of Hartfield is half way between them, about 8 miles from each. From Hartfield a road runs due south, the road to the coast. It goes up a steep hill and then down on the other side, and just before it reaches the bottom and crosses a little river there is a lane off to the right. As we made our weekly journey from

[1] See p. 1
[2] Now the 1/50,000 sheet 188.

54

London, this was the exciting moment. The car slowed down, almost stopped, then swung into the lane and our smooth motion changed into the familiar, welcoming, beloved bumping. For the lane was no more than a sandy track, well rutted by the wooden, iron-rimmed wheels of farm carts. In winter the ruts filled with water and we slooshed as well as bumped. I loved it. It was just how it should be: a proper country lane. My parents liked it this way, too: the bumpier it was the less likely were people to want to build houses along it. Only Burnside grumbled. "Jolly old lane," he said.

Cotchford Farm is a couple of hundred yards along on the left, a steep gravel drive leading down to it. We never knew its history, just spoke vaguely of Queen Anne and of its having once been three separate houses now turned into one, which accounted for its odd shape. We never knew it as a working farm, though various outbuildings survived, owned by a neighbouring farmer, and were still used in a half-hearted sort of way. It came to us through a man called Jervis who had rescued it, done it up and then sold it. And with it went two fields that took our boundaries up to the main road and along the river.

So there we were in 1925 with a cottage, a little bit of garden, a lot of jungle, two fields, a river and then all the green, hilly countryside beyond, meadows and woods, waiting to be explored; and Nanny and I set out at once to explore them, bringing back reports of our discoveries.

First we set off towards the river. We called it the river, though it was really only a stream, to distinguish it from the stream (at the bottom of the putting lawn) which was really only a long thin, almost stagnant pond. We were proud of our river. It was, we told our friends, a tributary of the Medway. This seemed to emphasise our remoteness from London. Not a tributary of the Thames: a tributary of the Medway; much grander, much more countrified. It was fringed all along by trees, mostly alders, and quite large ones, so that at a distance, looking towards it from the house, people could be excused for mistaking it for a wood. "Is that the Hundred Acre Wood?" they asked. You didn't discover that it was a river until you were right on top of it, for it had carved itself a deep channel through the red-brown, sandy-clay soil. If you climbed down to the water's edge you were quite invisible from the meadow above you. Here the air was cool and richly scented. The water, brown and mysterious, moved with unhurried dignity. It was just the right width: too wide to jump, but where a kindly tree reached out a branch to another kindly tree on the opposite shore, it was possible to swing yourself over. It was just the right depth: too deep to paddle across but often shallow enough to paddle in and in places deep enough to swim.

This was the river that Nanny and I set out to explore, and immediately we made our first discovery: Dragon's Bridge. There could be no doubt about it; for there was the great, blunt snout raised above the bank; there was the eye, round, hollow, staring; there was the branching wing, ready to beat the air; there was the leg poised above the water; and there was the great, green, scaly back down which you could – ("Do you think I dare, Nanny?" "Be very careful, dear.") – down which you could, if you were very careful, clamber until you were right across to the other side. Dragon's Bridge. This became and remained one of my favourite spots, the site of so many small adventures and happy memories. It was here that I built my hut of ash poles and bracken, here that I had my rope ladder (fastened to a giant oak tree that had perhaps sprung from one of the dragon's very own acorns), here that I launched my raft on its ten yard voyage, and here that I swam with Anne. Four strokes was all we could manage before we ran aground or got mixed up with a bramble, and even on the hottest day the water was achingly cold. . . .

And it must have been here that, in the poem, "Us Two", Pooh and I

... crossed the river and found a few—
"Yes, those are dragons all right," said Pooh.
"As soon as I saw their beaks I knew ..."

For on the other side of Dragon's Bridge was a chicken farm.

Two hundred yards or so upstream from Dragon's Bridge is the fence that marks our boundary. Who owned the land that lay beyond? Mostly we didn't know. Mostly we didn't care. As far as Nanny and I were concerned it belonged to us, and we never met anyone to contradict us. We wandered freely from field to field, from wood to wood, and scarcely met a soul.

On the other side of our fence is a hazel copse where wood anemones grow and where a tiny stream – a tributary of the tributary of the Medway – could be dammed or diverted or made to turn a miniature water wheel. Beyond the copse is a marsh, a tangled mass of rushes and bracken where only the gum-booted dare leave the path. It was here that, towards the end of one Easter holiday, to my enormous excitement, I finally tracked down the snipe's nest I had been searching for. At the end of the marsh the footpath crosses over the river above a weir, a plank spanning the water at the point where it curls smoothly over and crashes into the darkness, and a pole giving the nervous something to hold on to (and the daring something to swing on). On the other side is a good field for butterflies where blues and coppers could usually be found. Here I once came upon a weasel family out for a walk, and watched fascinated as mother weasel escorted her children to the edge of a little backwater and then, with much chattering and fussing, ferried them to the far side. The path follows the river bank and soon enters a wood. This is Posingford Wood and is marked on the map. So just in case, map in hand, you are trying to follow me, I must remind you that the countryside I am describing is the countryside I wandered in as a boy somewhere between 1925 and 1940. It didn't change much in those fifteen years, but it may have done so since.

Posingford was a wood we often used to visit. It is about half a mile from end to end and runs uphill from the river at the bottom to the Forest at the top. It is a gay and friendly wood, the sort of wood you could happily walk through at night, feeling yourself a skilful rather than a brave explorer: a wood of hazels and willows and sweet chestnuts with here and there an oak or a pine.

To the left of the path as it enters the wood is a lake. If you called our river a stream then I suppose you would want to call this lake a bog. But for me it was a lake: in winter when it froze over it was possible to do some quite good sliding between the tussocks of rush. The path continues between lake and river until it is crossed by a larger track that has entered the wood over a bridge. This bridge still stands and still looks much as it did when Shepard came there to draw it: it is Pooh-sticks Bridge.

It is difficult to be sure which came first. Did I do something and did my father then write a story around it? Or was it the other way about, and did the story come first? Certainly my father was on the look-out for ideas; but so too was I. He wanted ideas for his stories, I wanted them for my games, and each looked towards the other for inspiration. But in the end it was all the same: the stories became a part of our lives; we lived them, thought them, spoke them. And so, possibly before, but certainly after that particular story, we used to stand on Pooh-sticks Bridge throwing sticks into the water and watching them float away out of sight until they re-emerged on the other side.

Pooh-sticks Bridge was the way into Posingford if you came along the lane. The lane that takes you to Cotchford continues on to Upper Hartfield. Half way along its length it bends round to the right and at this point a track leads down hill to the left and this is the track you want. This was certainly the easier way, the way Nanny and I used to come. The other way, boggier and bramblier, was the way I preferred when I was rather older, when Nanny had left and I was on my own, when I was on the lookout for wild life and didn't want to meet people. Not that you were likely to meet many people if you did choose the lane. In fact the only person Nanny and I would be likely to meet was Hannah, and we would probably be looking for her anyway. She was a little older than I and lived in a house near Posingford where her father kept a chicken farm. A small child needs another child to play with. In London I had Anne, and there were lots of other friends living nearby whom I could meet from time to time. It is true that Anne often came to Cotchford (bringing her Nanny but leaving her parents behind); but she couldn't be there all the time that I was, and so I needed someone else; and luckily there was Hannah, only half a mile away. I cannot remember either how or where we first met. Probably we just happened on each other on one of our walks up the lane, and Nanny, who was good at talking to the people we met, talked to her, and that was how it all started. Our meetings were almost exclusively out of doors. We never went into Hannah's house, except just to call for her, and she never came to ours. We played in the woods and in the fields. We climbed trees and pretended to be monkeys. We paddled in the river and dug a hole in the river bank and called it the Channel Tunnel. We played in the barn and the stables that had once been part of Cotchford. We helped with the haymaking and rode home on the top of the hay cart. We helped with the apple picking and were allowed to eat the windfalls.

The barn was still in use. It housed, among other things, a swallow's nest, a farm cart, a chaff cutter and a very original smell. And two cart horses lived in the stable. A little farther up the lane was the apple orchard, whose trees, old and bent, made wonderful climbing. It was here that I lost Roo. We had all – Nanny and I and the animals – spent the afternoon playing there; and on our return Roo was missing. We went back and searched and searched, but in vain. Opposite the orchard were the fields and woods we visited on our flower picking expeditions. This wood for primroses, the ash plantation for orchids, the larger wood beyond for bluebells, the top of that field, along the edge of the bracken, for cowslips. Primroses, bluebells, orchids, cowslips, violets and foxgloves: Nanny and I would gather whole basketsful. And it was here – more especially than anywhere else – I would find that splendour in the grass, that glory in the flower, that today I find no more.

And so we worked our way down the lane, exploring farther and farther afield, until we came to the track down to the left, the bridge over the river and Posingford Wood on the other side. And just as on our first visit to the river we had discovered Dragon's Bridge, so on our first visit to Posingford we met the charcoal burner. And while Nanny, good at talking to people, talked to him, I, good at listening, listened. And then we returned home full of our exciting adventure.

There can be no doubt which came first here.

> The charcoal burner has tales to tell
> He lives in the forest
> Alone in the forest . . .

A ten-year-old boy might well have asked what charcoal was – how it was made and what it was used for – might have asked to see the tools that were needed, and the pit where the wood was burnt, might have gone home eager to try making his own charcoal. But I was only five, too young and too shy to ask. Old enough only to listen, and to remember indelibly one thing only. "And he told us he had once seen a fox!"

And rabbits come up and they give him good morning . . .
And owls fly over and wish him goodnight . . .
Oh, the charcoal burner has tales to tell . . .

There is a path through Posingford Wood – Nanny and I soon found it – that takes you up to the Forest. In fact this is the quickest way of getting to the Forest if you don't just go up the main road. (And who would choose a main road in preference to a path through a wood?)

If you look at Ashdown Forest on the map you will see that it covers an area roughly triangular in shape, an equilateral triangle with sides about six miles long and with the towns of Forest Row, Crowborough and Maresfield at its corners. The bit we knew best lay half way along the side joining Forest Row and Crowborough. This was the bit we could reach on foot.

Perhaps at this point I should break off for a moment to explain to those who today go everywhere by car that in those days we didn't. Cars had been invented – oh, yes, it wasn't all that long ago – and we had one and we also had a chauffeur to go with it. But they both lived in London and returned there after we had been deposited. So while we were at Cotchford we had to rely mainly on our feet. If we wanted to catch a train or if my father wanted to go golfing, we could always ring up Mitchells, the garage in Upper Hartfield. If we wanted to go shopping in Tunbridge Wells (as we usually did round about my birthday) we could walk to Hartfield and catch a bus. Other than that, we walked. It was not until later that my father learnt to drive (taught by Burnside) and we kept a car permanently at Cotchford.

So if we wanted to go up the Forest we went on foot. And so did others: only those who could walk to the Forest went there. This meant that when we got there we had the Forest almost entirely to ourselves. And this, in turn, made us feel that it was *our* Forest and so made it possible for an imaginary world – Pooh's world – to be born within the real world. Pooh could never have stumped a Forest that was littered with picnic parties playing their transistor radios.

Anyone who has read the stories knows the Forest and doesn't need me to describe it. Pooh's Forest and Ashdown Forest are identical. We came there often and since it was more of a walk than a ramble these were frequently family occasions, the four of us in single file threading the narrow paths that run through the heather. For my father, as I have said, though a bad rambler, was a keen walker.

Cotchford lies in a valley. To the south beyond the river the land rises, steadily up and up, until you reach the Forest. Then up and up again until you reach the top of the Forest. And at the very top of the Forest is Gills Lap. I could see Gills Lap from my nursery window. You could see Gills Lap from a great many places for miles around – a clump of pines on the top of a hill. And of course you can see it as Shepard drew it in *The House at Pooh Corner*. In the book it is Galleon's Lap but otherwise it is exactly as described, an enchanted spot before ever Pooh came along to add to its magic.

A path from Gills Lap takes you to the main road. On the other side the Forest falls away to a valley, then rises again beyond to distant trees. At the bottom of this valley runs a little stream. It is only a very little stream, narrow enough to jump across, shallow enough to paddle across, but it twists and tumbles between steep stony banks. It was here that the North Pole was discovered. As you make your way down to it and continue up on the other side you will be following the route Pooh took in an earlier chapter when he went "down open slopes of gorse and heather, over rocky beds of streams, up steep banks of sandstone into the heather again; and so at last, tired and hungry, to the Hundred Acre Wood" only, of course, as your map will have told you, it is really the Five Hundred Acre Wood.

The Five Hundred Acre is very different from Posingford. It is a real forest with giant beech trees, all dark and mysterious. You would indeed need to be a brave explorer to venture into the Five Hundred Acre at night, and I never did. The easiest way to get to it from Cotchford is down the main road past the Six Pine Trees, over the bridge, and then, a little farther on, through a gate on the left where a path leads to a farm on the top of a hill. On the other side of the hill a field runs down to a little stream. A bridge crosses the stream and beyond the bridge

3. Christopher and Pooh in the hollow tree

4a. Poohsticks Bridge: drawing by E. H. Shepard

4b. Poohsticks Bridge

the trees begin. Perhaps, to be accurate, I should say "began" because these trees vanished during the war. And this was sad for me, because among them was a tree I was particularly fond of. It was only just inside the wood and the path ran right by it. So Nanny and I must have discovered it on our first visit. It was a huge and ancient beech tree, one of a group of about half a dozen. It looked as if over the centuries it had grown tired of holding its arms up to the sky and had allowed its lower branches to droop. One branch in particular came out horizontally then curved downwards to rest its elbow on the ground. And at this point you could sit on it. Or you could stand on it and walk a little way along it and then jump off into the soft carpet of dead leaves spread out below. You could practise balancing, then practise jumping. It was difficult to walk very far for the branch was moss covered and slippery and soon got too steep, and there was nothing to hold on to. So then you could sit astride it and wriggle your way forward.

"Look, Nanny. Look how far I've got!"

"You mind you don't fall, dear."

"I'm all right."

I wriggled along the branch as far as I dared, until the ground seemed miles below me. If I had been braver I could have gone right the way along to where the branch joined the trunk. But it was a bit frightening. So I sat where I was, swinging my legs, then slithered back to safety. Then we went home to tea and to tell of our adventures and our discoveries.

"You must come and see it one day, come and watch me climb along it." And one day they did. One day all four of us visited the Five Hundred Acre to see the great tree, one to climb it, three to watch. And of those who watched, one perhaps to dream, to see the branch snaking to the ground and someone walking up it, walking easily, walking all the way, up the steep bit, along the level bit, right up to the trunk, finding there a door with a knocker and a bell, a door in the tree and someone living behind it. Who? Who? Could it be an owl? Could it be Owl that the visitor had come to see?

"And so at last, tired and hungry, to the Hundred Acre Wood. For it was in the Hundred Acre Wood that Owl lived."

I cannot swear that this was how it happened. It is only a guess. All I can say is that, though Owl was an imaginary character, invented by my father, his house was real. And this was it.

CHAPTER 9

Tree Houses

Posingford, the Forest, the Five Hundred Acre: this was where it all happened, but not where it started. It started much nearer home: at the top of the garden, in an ancient walnut tree. The tree was hollow inside and a great gash in its trunk had opened up to make a door. It was the perfect tree house for a five year old. I could climb inside and sit on the soft, crumbly floor. In the walls were cracks and ledges where things could be put; and high above my head was a green and blue ceiling of leaves and sky. Pooh and I claimed it. It was Pooh's House, really, but there was plenty of room for us both inside, and here we came to play our small, quiet, happy games together.

But though there was plenty of room for a boy and his bear, there wasn't enough room in it for Anne as well. She could come visiting, come to tea perhaps. But she couldn't live here. So she had to have another house, and luckily there was one: there was the well house. This was not the old well down at the bottom of the hill, but a new one we had had dug at the top just next to the walnut tree, to supply the Taskers' cottage. The water was deep down and safely covered over and above it was fixed a pump (a hand pump, of course); and over the whole thing was a wooden shed. This was where Anne lived. It was not such an exciting house as mine, but it was roomier. And so, though Anne could come to visit me, I usually went to visit her, and on her flatter, larger, more convenient floor we could prepare our mud pies, have our tea parties, sing our songs and laugh at each other's jokes.

Between our houses was a small path made of crazy paving. At first it didn't start anywhere very special or go anywhere very special. It was just a piece of crazy paving because a kind old man called Mr. Farmer had come to make crazy paving paths through our rock garden. I used to watch him, silently, intently, as small boys do. I watched him lay his sand base, then fit the stones together on top, then brush and water more sand into the gaps between them. It looked quite easy, something I could do too. So I was allowed to have some of his smallest stones, the bits that were no use to him, and I carried them up to Pooh's House, and built my path. Later I felt that it ought to go somewhere, so Tasker made me a wooden sundial. And then I felt anxious that perhaps too many people might walk down it to see the time and not do it any good. So I dug a heffalump trap at the other end and carefully disguised it with sticks and grass. And one day I caught Mrs. Tasker's foot, and was in disgrace.

Pooh's House was the first of many tree houses that I lived in on and off over the next few years, but it was the only one I could get right inside. The others were mostly apple trees or hazels.

"Hullo. What are you doing up there?"

"I'm in my bedroom. I've only just got up. But I'm coming down to my dining-room for breakfast. That's my dining-room, that branch down there."

To grown-ups one room looked much like another, for I made no attempt to furnish them, and I suppose I ought to have forgiven Tasker when, tidying up one day with his pruning saw, he sawed my dining-room down.

So if anyone wonders why in the stories so much time seems to be spent in trees or up trees, the answer is that this, in real life, was how it was.

CHAPTER 10
Weathers

"It rained and it rained and it rained." . . . In London if it was raining, you took a bus instead of walking to wherever it was you were going. Or you put on a macintosh instead of a coat. If it was raining Anne and I could spend the afternoon playing in the Natural History Museum instead of Kensington Gardens. It didn't make much difference to what we had planned to do. For if we didn't do it here, we could equally well do it there; and anyway most of the really exciting things were done indoors. But in the country it was quite different.

This was one of the things we discovered when we went to live at Cotchford. In the country the weather matters. In London you only notice the weather when it is very hot or very cold or very wet. But in the country there is weather every day; and sometimes it brings new and exciting things you can do, and sometimes it stops you doing the exciting things you had hoped to do.

Take the wind, for example. In London it came only on windy days, gusting down the street, throwing dust in your face as it passed. Maybe in the parks and along the river the trees fluttered their leaves and nodded their heads to it. But in the streets the lampposts stood unmoved like guardsmen on parade, the houses stared unblinking at the houses on the other side, cars and buses went on their way. Only when it got really angry and sent an old gentleman's hat bowling along the pavement did people stop and look.

But in the country there was wind not just on windy days but every day, even though it might be so gentle that only the poplar behind the rose garden noticed its passing. There was the wind that played over summer meadows; the wind that brought the hot scent of hay or the cool sweet scent of bracken; the wind that blew the cherry blossom down like snow, the wind that sent dead leaves scurrying and dancing down the road; the wind that carried the sound of church bells over the hills on a summer's evening to fill me with a strange sadness. There was the biting cold east wind that came out of a blue sky early in the new year, so that from indoors it looked as if spring had arrived and outdoors Nanny made me wear an overcoat. I hated wearing overcoats in the country, especially when it was so nearly spring. Overcoats were Londony things. Or there was the rollicking west wind, driving the clouds before it, roaring and tearing over the meadow, hurling itself at the trees, wailing in the telephone wires, hooting down the chimney, banging at the doors. "Come out, come out," it bellowed. And when I was out in it and alone in it I could shout back: "Blow harder, blow harder."

Or rain. Rain falling from a grey sky seen through my bedroom window just as it was getting light. Weather matters so much in the country, especially when you are young. I had been planning something special for today, something that needed the sun, and I had gone to bed the evening before all impatient with dull night, all eager for the morning. And now it was raining. I stood at the open window, staring up at the grey sky, staring and staring, trying to stare through the grey curtain to the blue that lay on the other side, trying to stare a hole in the curtain. "Red sky at night, shepherds' delight."

Last night had been so lovely and clear, and there had been a red sky as the sun had gone down, flooding the courtyard and dining-room with golden light. How could it be so different today? "Rain before seven, fine before eleven." My father had taught me that. Well, it was raining now and it was not yet seven. So there was a hope, quite a good hope really. I went back to bed, saying "Rain before seven, fine before eleven" over and over again to try and make it so.

But sometimes I liked the rain. "It rained and it rained and it rained" and little by little the level of the water in the stream rose until it was peering over the top. Then it began to creep up the putting lawn. . . . The stream that was really only a moat was now indeed a stream. The water was racing in through the little tunnel under the bridge at the top end, and piling up against the little tunnel under the other bridge at the bottom end. Perhaps I ought to put on Wellington boots and a macintosh and go and poke a stick through to clear it. Perhaps I might go down to the river to see what was happening. . . . Exciting! The river which usually ran, brown and peaceful, between high banks, was now only a few feet from the top, and fairly swirling and frothing and bubbling and seething and roaring along. Alders which grew at the edge of the water were now marooned on islands in mid stream, a fierce current racing between them and the mainland. The place where a tree root held back the river to make a waterfall – a sort of miniature, natural weir – could hardly be found, for the water below and the water above had both risen to the same level. I explored all along, then returned home to report. And still it rained. And it was still raining when I went to bed. And now I hoped that it would go on raining, and that when dull night was out of the way, I would wake up to find it coming down as hard as ever. Once again I rushed to the window as soon as I was awake. But I could hear the rain beating on the glass and knew before I got there that all was well. My bedroom window faced north. I would have to go to the window in the passage if I was to see what I wanted to see. And from the passage window I saw it. The water was over the top, over the top of the river and coming towards us across the meadow, over the top of the stream, half way up the putting lawn, and already into the rose garden.

All morning I watched it – we all watched it – fascinated. And every now and then I went out with a stick to mark the place where the tide had reached, a line of sticks getting nearer and nearer to the steps up to the path that ran outside the drawing-room.

> Every morning he went out with his umbrella and put a stick in the place where the water came up to, and every next morning he went out and couldn't see his stick any more. . . .

But though it rained and rained and rained, and though the river and the stream joined hands and the entire meadow became a lake, and though the rose garden and the mauve garden disappeared, the floods never reached the house. The men who, centuries earlier, had chosen to build Cotchford at the bottom of the hill, knew what the river could do, knew the highest point it could reach and laid their foundations eighteen inches above it.

The wind roaring in the trees, roaring in the giant sycamore that grew in the lawn just outside my nursery window ("What would happen if the wind blew it down? Would it flatten the house, do you think?") The rain beating on the water and the river rising to meet it. The snow, a rare visitor, and so all the more exciting when it came. Misty days when Gills Lap vanished and it might be fun to see if you could get lost and then cleverly find yourself again. Sunny days when the trees were dark and heavy with leaf and the air was heavy with the scent of meadow-sweet and the river was almost asleep. These were the Cotchford weathers, new and exciting to me; and for my father, perhaps, awakening memories of country holiday weathers when he was a boy. These are the weathers you will meet in the books.

I am often asked if I can remember when the stories were first read to me. Who read them? And where? And what did I think of them? Oddly, I can remember virtually nothing. One incident only survives.

My mother and I were in the drawing-room at Cotchford. The door opened and my father came in. "Have you finished it?" "I have." "May we hear it?" My father settled himself in his chair. "Well", he said, "we've had a story about the snow and one about the rain, and one about the mist. So I thought we ought to have one about the wind. And here it is.

"It's called:

"IN WHICH PIGLET DOES A VERY GRAND THING "Half way between Pooh's house and Piglet's house was a Thoughtful Spot. . . ."

My mother and I, side by side on the sofa, settled ourselves comfortably, happily, excitedly, to listen.

CHAPTER 11

Animals Tame and
Animals Wild

Though at Decoy I was allowed to keep a rabbit, and though my only recollection of our holiday in Wales is of being shown a dead snake that Griffiths, the butler, had bravely slain, it was not until we came to Cotchford that animals really entered my life – never, I hope, to leave it.

We started with two dogs, fox terriers – and a great mistake, though I never knew whose. They stayed with us only slightly longer than the gardener after whom one of them was named. He too proved to be a great mistake. After that we went in for cats.

It was Tasker, I think, who produced the founder of the family, a small tortoiseshell kitten. It was shown to me and I was asked to name it. "His name," I said, "is Pinkle; but I shall call him Tattoo." So Tattoo it was; and since cats don't immediately need more than one name (though they may later acquire two or three), Pinkle was available when Tattoo had grown up, discovered herself to be a girl, and produced her first offspring.

> Tattoo was the mother of Pinkle Purr,
> A little black nothing of feet and fur;

After that, kittens flowed thick and fast, though we managed to hold the adult population down to four. Pinkle was the only one to travel with us up to London. The others stayed at Cotchford, looked after by Mrs Tasker, greeting us at weekends in the rather offhand way that cats do, but nevertheless glad to see us. I adored them, of course, and felt tremendously flattered when one of them sat on my lap or lay on my bed or knocked on my bedroom door in the morning. Looking back on them and comparing them to cats I have known since (our present gang, for instance) I am bound to say that they were a dullish lot really. The only remarkable thing about them – and I never realized this until years later – was that we could safely leave a joint of meat on the sideboard or a plate of fish-paste sandwiches on the tea tray without first carrying out a thorough search of the room and then locking and bolting all doors and windows. No one believes this when I tell them, but I'm sure it's true. How different from our present lot, on whose account we have had to devise *double* locks for our food cupboards.

The other early addition to the family was Jessica, a donkey, and no connection whatever with Eeyore, except that she lived in a field a little like Eeyore's. It was Nanny's job, helped by Tasker and slightly helped by me, to catch her and saddle her. Sometimes this was easy, sometimes not. Our first outing was a cautious trip up the lane where, with luck, nothing too disastrous could happen. And I can still recall the horrifying moment when Jessica stopped and her legs began to sag. I was snatched from her back and Nanny and I watched, appalled, as she crumpled up on the ground, then rolled on to her side, then on to her back, then kicked up her legs in the air and let out an ear-splitting bellow, then rolled – still bellowing – from side to side, then scrambled to her feet and waited for me to remount. But Nanny said: "I don't think you'd better, dear." And I didn't think I'd better, either. And we all three walked home.

On subsequent trips we knew what to expect, that it was just one of the things Jessica liked doing, and so, when her legs started sagging, I got off and waited until it was all over. Subsequent trips included our weekly visit to Hartfield, a mile away along the main road, up a steep hill, down a steep hill and in at the door of the first shop on the left hand side. Jessica needed no urging and the woman behind the counter no instructions. It was a pennyworth of bullseyes for each of us.

Other creatures came and went. Frog spawn made its annual appearance in a jam jar on the windowsill in my nursery. Hedgehogs were discovered, given lodgings, stayed for a while, then made their escape. Bantams laid an egg or two in the potting shed. Ducks swam on the stream until their wing feathers had grown. Pigeons coo-ed from the dovecot. A mouse squeezed himself between the floorboards in my bedroom and for a few happy days found a piece of cheese waiting for him. And Alexander Beetle lived briefly in a matchbox.

But though I made my wish, as Nanny told me I should, when I ate my first raspberries, and though I never told anybody what I had wished for, I never got the elephant, the real live elephant, that I had really set my heart on.

CHAPTER 12

The Toys

I must now introduce the toys.

Pooh was the oldest, only a year younger than I was, and my inseparable companion. As you find us in the poem "Us Two", so we were in real life. Every child has his favourite toy, and every only-child has a special need for one. Pooh was mine, and probably, clasped in my arms, not really very different from the countless other bears clasped in the arms of countless other children. From time to time he went to the cleaners, and from time to time ears had to be sewn on again, lost eyes replaced and paws renewed.

Eeyore, too, was an early present. Perhaps in his younger days he had held his head higher, but by the time the stories came to be written his neck had gone like that and this had given him his gloomy disposition. Piglet was a present from a neighbour who lived over the way, a present for the small boy she so often used to meet out walking with his Nanny. They were the three round which the stories began, but more characters were needed and so two were invented: Owl and Rabbit. Owl was owlish from the start and always remained so. But Rabbit, I suspect, began by being just the owner of the hole in which Pooh got stuck and then, as the stories went on, became less rabbity and more Rabbity; for rabbits are not by nature good organizers. Both Kanga and Tigger were later arrivals, presents from my parents, carefully chosen, not just for the delight they might give to their new owner, but also for their literary possibilities.

So there they were, and to a certain extent their characters were theirs from birth. As my father said, making it all sound very simple, you only had to look at them to see at once that Eeyore was gloomy, Piglet squeaky, Tigger bouncy and so on. But of course there was much more to it than that. Take bears, for example.

A row of Teddy bears sitting in a toyshop, all one size, all one price. Yet how different each is from the next. Some look gay, some look sad. Some look stand-offish, some look lovable. And one in particular, that one over there, has a specially endearing expression. Yes, that is the one we would like, please.

The bear took his place in the nursery and gradually he began to come to life. It started in the nursery; it started with me. It could really start nowhere else, for the toys lived in the nursery and they were mine and I played with them. And as I played with them and talked to them and gave them voices to answer with, so they began to breathe. But alone I couldn't take them very far. I needed help. So my mother joined me and she and I and the toys played together, and gradually more life, more character flowed into them, until they reached a point at which my father could take over. Then, as the first stories were written, the cycle was repeated. The Pooh in my arms, the Pooh sitting opposite me at the breakfast table, was a Pooh who had climbed trees in search of honey, who had got stuck in a rabbit hole, who was "a bear of no brain at all." . . .

Then Shepard came along, looked at the toy Pooh, read the stories and started drawing; and the Pooh who had been developing under my father's pen began to develop under

Shepard's pen as well. You will notice if you compare the early Poohs in *Winnie the Pooh* with the later Poohs in *The House at Pooh Corner*. What is it that gives Pooh his particularly Poohish look? It is the position of his eye. The eye that starts as quite an elaborate affair level with the top of Pooh's nose, gradually moves downwards and ends up as a mere dot level with his mouth. And in this dot the whole of Pooh's character can be read.

That was how it happened. And when at last the final story had been written, my father, looking back over the seven years of Pooh's life, wrote his dedication. It was to my mother.

> You gave me Christopher Robin, and then
> You breathed new life in Pooh.
> Whatever of each has left my pen
> Goes homing back to you.
> My book is ready, and comes to greet
> The mother it longs to see –
> It would be my present to you, my sweet,
> If it weren't your gift to me.

In the last chapter of *The House at Pooh Corner* our ways part. I go on to become a schoolboy. A child and his bear remain playing in the enchanted spot at the top of the forest. The toys are left behind, no longer wanted, in the nursery. So a glass case was made for them and it was fastened to the nursery wall in Mallord Street, and they climbed inside. And there they lived, sometimes glanced at, mostly forgotten, until the war came. Roo was missing. He had been lost years before, in the apple orchard up the lane. And Piglet's face was a funny shape where a dog had bitten him. During the war they went to America and there they have been ever since. . . .

If you saw them today, your immediate reaction would be: "How old and battered and lifeless they look." But of course they are old *and* battered *and* lifeless. They are only toys and you are mistaking them for the real animals who lived in the forest. Even in their prime they were no more than a first rough sketch, the merest hint of what they were to become, and they are now long past their prime. Eeyore is the most recognizable; Piglet the least. So, if I am asked "Aren't you sad that the animals are not in their glass case with you today?" I must answer "Not really," and hope that this doesn't seem too unkind. I like to have around me the things I like today, not the things I once liked many years ago. I don't want a house to be a museum. When I grew out of my old First Eleven blazer, it was thrown away, not lovingly preserved to remind me of the proud day I won it with a score of 13 not out. Every child has his Pooh, but one would think it odd if every man still kept his Pooh to remind him of his childhood. But my Pooh is different, you say: he is *the* Pooh. No, this only makes him different to you, not different to me. My toys were and are to me no more than yours were and are to you. I do not love them more because they are known to children in Australia or Japan. Fame has nothing to do with love.

I wouldn't like a glass case that said: "Here is fame"; and I don't need a glass case to remind me: "Here was love".

CHAPTER 13
Husky at Pageants

When I was about eight years old I spent a fortnight at Little-hampton-after-Whooping-Cough (as my mother used to call it, to distinguish it from Littlehampton-after-Chicken-Pox where I had gone the previous year). I went with Nanny, and since we stayed at the same boarding house on each occasion I find it difficult now to disentangle the two visits; but it was certainly on our second that I had riding lessons. I could ride Jessica, of course. That is to say I could sit on her broad back and be carried down to the village. But that wasn't real riding. That wasn't what I was learning to do now, for the first time, at Littlehampton-after-Whooping-Cough.

But this chapter is not about riding, although riding became then and remained for the next seven years or so my passion in life. I mention it for another reason, because of a remark that my riding instructor made that has stuck in my memory. I had asked if I could do something, I forget what, something more difficult, more daring, more exciting; and he had said, "No." Then he added: "You see I've got to take care of you. After all, you're quite an important little personage."

This chapter, then, is about being quite an important little personage.

The books were published and each as it appeared met with immediate and enormous success. The names of Pooh and Christopher Robin became known to thousands of children and their parents.

Throw a stone into a pool of water and you make a splash from which the ripples travel outwards. The bigger the splash, the further the ripples travel before they die away. Pooh made a big splash and the ripples travelled a long way. But a child has small horizons and they soon passed over the edge of mine and vanished out of sight. I had my own copies of the books, of course. I read them often (the stories more than the poems), knew them well and loved them greatly. My friends had their copies, and they liked them, as I would have expected. But if the books were also being read and enjoyed by complete strangers in Edinburgh and New York, this was something I knew nothing about. Were the reviews rapturous? Even if I had known, I could not have measured their rapture nor compared it with the rapture that had greeted other children's books. And even if I had been able to measure it, I would naturally have expected my father's books to be better than anyone else's. Was Bumpus reporting record sales? Was Methuen ordering reprint after reprint? What did I know of this? What would the figures have meant to me even if I had known them?

Most of the ripples, then, travelled over my horizon and away; so that a child in Los Angeles was better able to judge the fame of Pooh than I was. But some were reflected and came back; and of those that came back, some were allowed through my nursery door.

My nursery door. Was it left open or did they keep it shut? If shut, how carefully was it guarded? How many of all who hoped to come through were turned away? These are questions I never wondered about until now, and now it is too late to find the answers. I can only record my memories of what did get through. Letters, for a start, though probably not every letter. Today I still get letters from children asking after Pooh; so I imagine I got them then, though I cannot very vividly recall them. Perhaps they were mostly intercepted. If "Wol" was to be their answer, it was surely better and kinder to all that this decision should be my parents' rather than mine. So perhaps I was only allowed to read those that seemed extra nice, extra appealing, extra deserving, those where a reply really would bring pleasure outweighing the wearisomeness of writing: the letters from Farm Street School, for instance.

They came in a single large envelope. There must have been dozens of them, all in their different childish hands, a batch from the girls in Form 3A, a batch from the girls in Form 4B. . . . Some in pencil, some in pen, some with pictures, some without; and accompanying them, introducing them, explaining them, excusing them, putting in a word on their behalf, a letter from the Headmistress, Miss Craig. It only needed a single letter back to make all these girls happy, for Miss Craig would read it out to them and each would feel it was a letter to her personally in answer to the one that she herself had written.

"But what shall I say, Nanny?"

"I'll help you, dear. We'll think it out together. It doesn't have to be very long. I'm sure they'll be delighted with it."

And so I wrote. And they replied. And I wrote again. And somethimes, as I mentioned earlier, I said it with primroses; and once I nearly said it with a Bible. Miss Craig, Farm Street Girls School, Hockley, Birmingham: the only address that I have not written to for over 45 years that I can still recall.

Then there were the reporters. I imagine that here the door was guarded with extra vigilance. But two got through and one even managed a few brief words. The first, disguised perhaps as a Nanny, joined the Nanny spectators at Macpherson's gymnasium as they watched their small charges, marching, running, jumping and climbing. I may have been bad at marching but I was good at climbing, and this was what she noticed. Her words – when later I read them – were music in my ears; I glowed with pride. She had heard a tinkling sound coming from high up in the roof, she had looked up and seen me clinging to one of the ropes that hung from the ceiling, ringing the bell to prove that I had reached the top. And now she was telling the world that this was the sort of thing that Christopher Robin could do. O kind reporter, if you are yet alive and read this, may I thank you for the still remembered pleasure your words brought me.

The other reporter met me at Cotchford on the path that, running through the kitchen garden, led from the house to the lane. She was coming down it, having just arrived and for some reason using what was really the tradesmen's entrance. I was going up it on my way to find Hannah. She stopped in the middle of the path so that I couldn't get by, smiled and said "Good morning." Then she produced a watch that she had been carrying, told me that she had found it lying on the ground, and asked if it were mine. I looked at it. It was a cheap, toy watch, the sort of thing that might have come out of a cracker, now rather dirty and battered. I answered and went on my way, and she continued down towards the house and towards the interview that she had arranged with my father.

Some weeks later we saw the magazine in which her interview appeared. It was a longish one, but only the first paragraph was of any interest to me. In it she described our meeting on the path and the question she had put. And she gave my answer. And her words seared themselves indelibly into my memory. Was it my watch? "Yes, it is," she made me reply. "It's a good sort of watch but it doesn't quite go." I read this paragraph with amazement, indignation and rage. It was one of those moments, familiar to all of us, when illusion is shattered. There had been the occasion when, as we walked to school, Anne had destroyed my belief in Father Christmas. Now came the destruction of my faith that what people wrote about you was true. From that day on I never managed to feel quite the same about journalists: they had lost my confidence. And if now I am less polite, less co-operative towards them than they might wish, here is where it all started, here with this miserable woman, who made me quote one of my father's poems ("The Engineer", which, in any case, is not really about me at all), when what I actually said was: "No. It probably belongs to our gardener's daughter."

Then there was the play. This was adapted from the story of Eeyore's birthday. Because I was in it, and because I would naturally be taking the part of me, Owl (who appears in the story) had to become Christopher Robin (who doesn't). I still find this a little difficult to explain. I had to explain it to Mr. Gibbs, the headmaster of my day school in London, when he wanted to stage the same little play: and it was a long time before I could be quite certain that he had my meaning and wasn't going to make me dress up in feathers.

Eeyore's Birthday with Christopher Robin playing the part of himself, Robert as Pooh, Ann[1] as Eeyore and Veronica as Piglet. A single public performance only; part of a "charity matinee". I cannot remember, if indeed I ever knew, what else the audience was to get for its money. Our little bit was all that mattered to us. We rehearsed it and rehearsed it, then did it, then went home. With my father a playwright and Ann's mother an actress we could at least claim that we were professionally produced even if our acting was amateur and the leading player's only previous connection with the stage had been in the part of Sir Andrew Aguecheek. If any memory of this little play survives anywhere today, it will be a memory of Piglet. For it was she who stole the show; Piglet, the smallest and youngest of us all; Piglet, with her sing-song, slightly cold-in-the-nose voice (just like her mother's); Piglet, pink-faced and adorable; Piglet, aged four.

[1] Not Anne Darlington. Another Ann.

"Yes, but I'm afraid – I'm very sorry, Eeyore – but when I were running along to bring it to you, I fell down . . ."

But unfortunately the balloon didn't always burst and Piglet was left rolling about on top of it, pinching it, punching it, getting crosser and crosser, pinker and pinker. It was her Nanny, the ever-watchful, closely attending "Bun", who knew the answer and produced it from behind her white apron. "Here, Veronica, use this pin." And so she did; and though at some rehearsals the explosion was disconcertingly premature, and though her appearance on stage, dashing across the floor, large balloon clasped to tummy, was always attended with some anxiety, on the great afternoon the timing was perfect. And I can remember not only my feeling of relief but also my admiration at the competent way she disposed of the pin once its duty had been done. With a graceful flick of the wrist she sent it skimming over the boards to the feet of Bun waiting in the wings.

Then there was the gramophone record. My father had already made one. His was a reading from chapter 3 of *Winnie the Pooh*. "The Piglet lived in a very grand house . . ." He had a dry, monotonous voice. No ups and downs. If you had commented on this he would have said that the words spoke for themselves. If they were good words (and they *were* good words because he had chosen them) they spoke well and didn't need any acting, any special straining for effect on the part of the reader. Partly this was true, and certainly too little expression is far better than too much; but partly my father just did have a rather dry, quiet, toneless voice, and couldn't help it. My mother was the family's reader. And when it was my turn to make a gramophone record it was on her that I modelled myself.

My pieces were from the poems, three of them were sung, one was recited. Fraser-Simson, who had written the music, was going to accompany me on the piano; and his wife, Cicely, being a singer, would help me make the best of what voice I then had. For I was only about 7 years old at the time. I had only just left "On the grassy banks"; solos and descants in school chapel were still four years away.

So, after some preliminary rehearsals in the drawing-room at Mallord Street under my mother, we went round, my father, my mother and I, to the Fraser-Simson's house for a final practice before going on to the H.M.V. studio.

Fraser-Simson was a rather fierce-looking man with a great grey moustache. His name was Harold but we knew him only as F-S. Cicely was much younger and gay and pretty and I liked her. But best of all I liked Henry Woggins, their spaniel. And so while the grown-ups were having their grown-up talk sitting in elegant chairs, Henry Woggins and I were on the floor and I was telling him all about what was going to happen.

"Well, Christopher, are you ready? Shall we try the first one?" I got up, feeling a little dry in the mouth, and F-S. walked over to his piano. The introductory bars . . . a deep breath, and Cicely brought me in:

> There are lots and lots of people who are always asking things,
> Like dates and pounds and ounces . . .

I reached the end and waited.

"Well done. That was very nice. . . . Just one or two little points. . . . I think it might be nice if you could manage a slightly Poohish voice when he answers: 'Well, I say six-pence. . . .' Then the music says 'and the names of fun-ny kings', but I'd like you to sing it like this. . . . And then here you'll want to take a really deep breath to last you through to the end of the line. . . . Shall we just try it once more?"

I liked being taught by Cicely. I tried again, remembering the things she had told me. "That's much better." Then I went through the other two songs. Of course I didn't have to sing them perfectly. I was a small boy not a professional. A little wobbling on the long notes, a little breathlessness at the end of the line wouldn't matter, might indeed add to the charm. . . . Anyway, time was getting on. We were due at the studio at half past three, the six of us. For Henry Woggins would be coming too, of course. He had never been to a recording studio before and so it would be a little alarming for him. But luckily I was going to be there to look after him. If he felt nervous at all, I would be there to stroke his ears. I did so hope that he would behave nicely so that I could feel proud of him. It was quite a responsibility for me. . . .

We got ourselves ready. We climbed into the car. We arrived. We were greeted and introduced. We were ushered along passages. We reached the studio door. The door was opened and we filed in, my mother and Cicely, my father and F-S. This was the great moment. From now on Henry Woggins would be on his own. Come on, it's our turn now. I stooped down to give him a reassuring pat.

"Enter well," I said. And to my great relief he did.

The pageant was at Kidbrooke Park on the edge of Ashdown Forest. The theme was "Ashdown Forest through the Centuries" – or something similar. The setting was a circular, saucer-like field lying within a crescent of trees. In the middle of the crescent was a gap where a track, coming from behind the trees on the right, swung out into the open, crossed a broad, flat wooden bridge, and so entered the stage. And down the track and over the bridge came Boadicea and the ancient Britons, came Henry VIII and his courtiers, came Anne Boleyn to her trial. Down the track galloped the Excise Men, the hooves of their horses echoing on the planks of the bridge. But the witch came in through the trees on the left, limping, ragged, white hair flying, long stick in hand. She was seized and bound and carried off to be burned at the stake. And as she went she pointed to the castle that could be dimly seen among the trees, raised her stick and cursed ...

So the pageant went its memorable way, and I see it now like an ancient ciné film, much faded and blurred and with many breaks, but with here and there a sequence as vivid as the day it was shot. On it went through the centuries until we had reached the present. Ashdown Forest today. This is my bit. After the splendours and the drama of the past, the simplicity of the present. A tiny child coming down through the trees, quite alone, but carrying something. What is it? His toys. Yes, of course, his famous toys! Slowly the child makes his way over the grass towards the far side. Half way across he drops something, doesn't notice at once, walks on a few paces, then stops and looks back. Yes, it was Eeyore. It would be Eeyore! He goes back, picks him up, and continues his long journey. And now he is in among the trees and out of sight. A pause. Look, now he's coming back. Not carrying anything this time. Back into the field again. But this time he is not alone. Behind him come the animals, grown larger, walking one behind the other. Pooh, Piglet, Eeyore, Tigger, Kanga. . . . In the middle of the field the child stops and holds up his hand. One by one the others come up, form a circle round him and sit down. . . . This is Ashdown Forest today, where a boy and his bear will always be playing. . . .

And so the pageant ends; and while Christopher Robin and his animals are having their picnic, those who had tramped the Forest in bygone days reappear in a great procession, down the track, over the bridge and round the field, Ancient Britons, Knights in Armour, Henry VIII and Anne Boleyn, the witch, the Excise Men ... and as the tail of the column passes him Christopher Robin stands up. The picnic is over. Time to go home. Come on. And he and his animals tag on to the end of the line, round the field and out through the trees. . . .

That was the pageant. I was about nine years old at the time and it was immensely exciting to be in it. Exciting without being frightening. For there was nothing to be nervous about, nothing to go wrong. It was not like acting in a play or making a gramophone record when your voice might go funny. It was exciting doing my bit, exciting watching all the other bits and exciting to feel that I was part of it all, me and Henry VIII. . . . So although I was to come on last I was able to enjoy all the earlier scenes. I could watch them from the front, or I could wander around the back. And sometimes, wandering round the back, I would come upon groups of Courtiers waiting their turn to go on. And once I came upon the witch. She was sitting under a tree, glasses on her nose, reading a newspaper; and she was smoking a pipe. It gave me quite a little shock. I never expected to see a witch smoking a pipe.

Then, as the centuries rolled towards the present, I collected my toys together and Nanny and I made our way to the place where I was to come on. Got everything?

"Got your handkerchief?"

"Yes, Nanny." I cleared my throat.

"Do you want to blow your nose?"

"No, I don't think so." I cleared my throat again.

"You're not getting a cold, I hope." Nanny looked at me anxiously.

"No, I'm all right." I cleared my throat once more.

Then, feeling an explanation was called for:

"I'm *always* husky at pageants."

CHAPTER 14

The Busy Backson

On January 15th, 1929 – the only date that has survived from my childhood unforgotten – wearing my new, bright red blazer and my bright red, rather large and loose-fitting peaked cap, with my hair of a length which, if not exactly boyish, was at least no longer girlish, at half past eight in the morning and accompanied by Nanny, I climbed onto a number 11 bus at the corner of Church Street, bound for Sloane Square and my first day at Gibbs. Four hours later I was home again and in my father's library, telling him all about it, telling him about the thing that had impressed and amazed me most.

"We have to call Mr. Gibbs 'Sir'."

"Sir" was what Gertrude called my father, what servants called their masters, what people who worked called the people they worked for, not what boys like me had to call anybody, surely. I expected my father to be as amazed and indignant as I was, and was even more amazed when he wasn't. Gently he explained to me that schoolboys did address schoolmasters as "Sir", that he had done so when he was a boy and that now I must. Gently he reassured me. . . . And thus we reached a small landmark in our lives. For me it marked the full realization of the newness and strangeness of the world I had just entered; for my father the first of many opportunities to help me on my way through it.

Gibbs was – indeed it still is – a boys' day school. It was then at the bottom of Sloane Street and Mr. C. H. Gibbs was its headmaster. It took boys from the age of about six to the age of thirteen. I arrived at eight-and-a-half, stayed for four terms, then went on to boarding school. Gibbs for me was therefore a bridge between kindergarten and prep school, between Miss Walters and Boxgrove, between Plasticine and raffia on the one hand and Latin declensions and simultaneous equations on the other. It was a bridge between childhood and boyhood, between the nursery world of Nanny and the drawing-room world of my parents, between the years in which I could identify myself with the Christopher Robin in the books and the years spent trying to escape from him. And since my arrival at Gibbs also marks the halfway point in this book, it is perhaps a good moment to pause and look back.

At Gibbs I was still living in the nursery. Nanny was still very much at the centre of my life. She took me there every morning and was waiting in the hall to take me home at the end of the day. She came to the lantern lectures we had every Tuesday afternoon and helped me with the essays I had to write about them the following weekend. She prompted me with:

Lars Porsena of Cluseum, by the nine gods he swore. . . .

and

I stood tiptoe upon a little hill . . .

She read me *The Heroes of Asgard* and *Great Expectations*. And, perhaps most important of all, she accompanied me on my visits to James Greig, the ironmonger in Sloane Square. For among the many new things I was learning at my new school – *mensa* and *amo*, the dates of George I, the shape of North

America: none of them in later life to prove particularly useful – was one that was worth more than all the others put together. Once a week I did carpentry. Once a week I sawed and chiselled and sand-papered; and so once a week (or thereabouts) I told Nanny what it was I wanted and together we went to James Greig to get it. Nanny did the asking (she was better at asking than I was) and I searched in my trouser pockets for the money. With Nanny's help and encouragement I became a carpenter, with my own private carpenter's shop in the attic at Cotchford. And I have remained a carpenter ever since.

But if Nanny was still with me, Pooh was moving into the shadows. For seven and a half years he had been my constant companion; now our ways were beginning to part. "GON· OUT BACKSON BISY BACKSON" said the notice on the piece of paper. I was now living in two worlds. In one of them we could perhaps still meet for a little longer, but in the other I was on my own. We had had a happy time together. The imaginary world we inhabited was very much the world you meet in the stories. Our real world was the sort of real world you would expect to find lying behind them. I loved my Nanny, I loved Cotchford. If I cannot say that I loved my parents it is only because, in those early days, I just didn't know them well enough. And if I do not say that I loved Mallord Street, it is only because I loved Cotchford so very much more.

I also quite liked being Christopher Robin and being famous. There were indeed times – as at pageants – when it was exciting and made me feel grand and important. But of the ripples of fame that came through my nursery door, each was judged firmly on its merits. A child loves getting presents at Christmas, loves opening parcels, but he becomes instantly critical once the brown paper and string are off. The double-barrelled shotgun is wonderful and just exactly what he wanted; the large rubber ball is rather stupid. The rubber ball is left on one side and instantly forgotten (except by Nanny who has thoughtfully noted down that it was sent by Aunt Mary), the shotgun is borne off to the nursery and the instructions are eagerly read and puzzled out. It was the same with the Christopher Robin things. If, in the watercolour painting by Honor Maugham, I looked sad, this was because I was sad. The sun was shining, Hannah had come round to play with me and was hanging about outside waiting, and here I was indoors having to sit still.

When I was about eight years old, being fond of animals I was not surprisingly a Dr. Dolittle fan; and one day I wrote to Hugh Lofting to say so. Partly I wrote because Nanny encouraged me to, partly I wrote because I really did want to say how much I liked the books, and I suppose that partly I wrote because I hoped I might get a letter back And I did; and I was thrilled when he asked me which of his books I had not read so that he could send me copies. Kind Mr. Lofting to give a small boy so much pleasure. Was the small boy always as kind to those who wrote to *him*? Would he, as he grew older, become kinder or less kind? If the answer to the second question is "Less kind" this is because there is a difference between being an author and being a character in a book. The author remains the author always. The character may well grow out of his part. At the age of seven I was quite pleased when a large "Piglet" arrived in a box with his creator's best wishes. He was much more handsome, indeed frankly much more appealing and lovable, than my one (who was anyway by this time in a rather dog-bitten state). I christened him Poglet and he and Pooh accompanied me on one of my visits to Littlehampton. But had he arrived five years later his welcome would have been cooler. Anyone wanting to make toy Piglets to send to the little boy in the book had to study the back of the title page to be sure that the little boy was still a little boy. Miss B. was really too late. Miss B. produced a Pooh and a Piglet modelled in clay. Forty years later she discovered that she still had my thank-you letter and sent me a copy of it to ask if I thought it was worth anything. I replied that I hoped not; anyway it wasn't to me. But on second thoughts I feel I may be mistaken. It is perhaps just worth printing as the only contemporary document that survives to give the true flavour of a Christmas holiday when I was 12 years old.

> Dear Miss B. . . .
> Thank you so much for Pooh and Piglet. I did love them so, and I love having them with me. They weren't too tired out with the journey although Piglet broke his arm; however he is all right now.
> I am playing cricket (net practice) nearly every day here. Every weekend we go down to the country: I can go on long explores in the forest and up to Gills Lap (Galleon's Lap). We have four cats in the country, but although they are very common they are awfully friendly and go to sleep on your knee. Their mother who is about 7 or 8 years old has had at least 60 or 70 kittens 50 of which had to be drowned. We have in our country house two so-called secret passages. Unfortunately I am the only one who can get into them but I have great fun furnishing them, wall-papering them and putting up electric bells and lights. This is very grand because my room (or passage) is the only one which has electric lights or bells.
> My mother has just come back from New York. The boat arrived a day late though and left her only two days for her Christmas shopping.
> I do hope you have a very happy new year
> > with very best love from
> > CHRISTOPHER ROBIN MILNE
> P.S. Excuse bad writing.

It was not entirely Miss B's fault that she was five years late Every year brings its new batch of readers, meeting Christopher Robin and Pooh for the first time, learning that maybe Christopher Robin is a real live person and expecting him still to look like his picture. Even if you are wise enough to realize that the books were written a long time ago and that real live people grow up, you may still find yourself judging them by today's standards. It is easy to see that some of the verses in *When We Were Very Young* are now rather out of date. Nannies in uniforms are now more or less extinct. But attitudes as well as people change. If today's reader detects an air of snobbishness and class consciousness here and there it would be unfair to blame the author for this. My father was writing in the 1920s about the 1920s to entertain people living in the 1920s and these were the attitudes current at the time. Yet if Christopher Robin seems a rather odd little boy, in one respect he is now less odd than he once was. Today his long hair and curious clothes are very much in fashion. But at the time, when other little boys had short hair, shirts and ties, they were decidedly unusual. Was this Shepard's idea, or my father's – or whose?

First let me say that it had nothing to do with Shepard. It is true that he used his imagination when he drew the animals, but me he drew from life. I did indeed look just like that. And the reason I looked like that had nothing whatever to do with the books either. What the reason was I can only now guess. At the time I accepted it as I accepted nursery food. It was just part of life. And I was that sort of child: the sort that accepts things without question. Later on, when I was older, I might perhaps have asked; but a tactful moment combined with a sufficient interest in learning the answer never presented itself. And it is not really until today that I have found myself wondering. Too late now to know for sure, and so I must just try to piece together such clues as survive.

When a child is small it is his mother who is mainly responsible for the way he is brought up. So it was with me. I belonged in those days to my mother rather than to my father. He was busy writing. It was she who gave the instructions to

Nanny. And so it was she who found the patterns and provided the material (leaving Nanny to do the actual sewing). It was she who outlined the hair-style (leaving Nanny to do the actual scissor-work). This I know. All the same, there could well have been consultation and discussion in the drawing-room – while I was in bed and Nanny was busy with the ironing – before decisions were made and orders were given. This I don't know. But I suspect that the result appealed equally to both my parents – though for quite different reasons. I suspect that, with my golden tresses, I reminded my mother of the girl she had always wanted to have. And I would have reminded my father of the boy with long, flaxen hair he once had been. Each reason – as I hope to show – would have been in character. And the second provides the key that unlocks the secret of the Pooh books.

CHAPTER 15
Another Portrait

In May 1930 I said goodbye to Nanny. I was nearly ten years old. She had been with me for over eight years. Apart from her fortnight's holiday every September we had not been out of each other's sight for more than a few hours at a time. Even when I had gone to hospital to have my tonsils out she had come with me. I was also saying a temporary goodbye to home, for I was off to Boxgrove School near Guildford and would be spending the next three months in a strange place among strange people.

Life at a boarding school is so very different from home life that the only way some boys can cope with it is to become two boys. They split themselves down the middle and become a schoolboy at school, reverting to home-boy during the holidays. This, I suspect, is particularly true of introspective boys, such as I was. Indeed in my case the split was particularly deep. For it was now that began that love-hate relationship with my fictional namesake that has continued to this day. At home I still liked him, indeed felt at times quite proud that I shared his name and was able to bask in some of his glory. At school, however, I began to dislike him, and I found myself disliking him more and more the older I got. Was my father aware of this? I don't know. Certainly this must have been an anxious period for him. Up to now my mother had been mainly responsible for me. Now it was his turn. He had made me a name, more of a name than he had really intended. How much of a help would this prove to be? Or how much of a hindrance?

On the last day of the holidays the pattern was always the same. We were back in London. My father went to the Garrick Club in the morning. I lunched alone with my mother. After lunch she read aloud to me in the drawing-room. At about three o'clock my father returned. Burnside came in for my trunk and loaded it on to the car. I changed into my school clothes and said goodbye to my mother. She never came with me. The journey to school was always with my father alone. We did *The Times* crossword, then sat silent. School was all right when I got there, but home was so very much nicer, and these journeys, three of them every year for nine years, were as sorrowful for me as the three annual journeys in the opposite direction (by train) were blissful.

We said our goodbyes while still in the car and while there was still a mile or two to go. We said them looking straight ahead. It was easier that way. The goodbye I said to my father was different from the one I had said an hour earlier to my mother. Hers was goodbye until the next holidays. His was only a partial goodbye; for part of him would be remaining with me, hovering over me, lovingly and anxiously watching me, throughout the term. It was he, not she, who got something done about the draughty classroom at Gibbs and the over-crowded changing-room at Stowe – (and, many years later, about a military hospital at Bari). It was he, far more often than she, who used to visit me on visiting days; he who knew the masters; he who could chat happily and naturally to the other boys.

But first we had to get to know each other, and a vivid picture still remains with me of his first visit to Boxgrove during my first term. This was one of those rare occasions when my mother came too. It was a Wednesday afternoon. There was a cricket match on and I was watching it from the bottom of the field. Then a message came down to me: "Your parents have arrived"; and I hurried back up the hill towards the school. And then I saw them, side by side, coming towards me. How strange and unfamiliar they looked, how out of place in these surroundings. How little I felt I knew them. How little they seemed to be mine.

Maybe they felt the same about me. This quiet, small, serious-looking boy, wearing his curious school clothes, with his hair now so very short. Who is he? Are we going to like him?

During the next few years we were going to find out; and in the remaining chapters I am going to report what then, and later, was discovered. The first discoveries concern mainly my parents; the later ones myself. And we will begin with a very early – indeed a pre-school – discovery about my father.

How much does a child ever know about the adults he lives with? There are certain things they show him, either because they want to or because they can't help it, and there are certain other things they keep from him. Of all he sees, some he understands: of all he understands, some he remembers. And if what survives is worn and fragmented, he can, in later life, an adult now himself, do a little repair work. Now and in the chapters that follow I am not attempting more than this.

One of the first things a child discovers about a person is what he looks like – his face. My father's face was easiest in profile and so that was how I used to draw it. He came up to the nursery and sat, smoking his pipe, at one end of the nursery table, while I sat at the other. He sat and smoked and thought. I sat and drew and occasionally rubbed out. We both sat in silence. This was something we did from time to time, something we could do together on our first shy meetings.

My father was not an artist. Nor was I, though there were hopes in those early days that I might eventually become one. My father was good at writing. How nice if one day I were equally good at drawing. Drawing rather than writing. You wouldn't want to have two writers in the family; for then people might say that the son was not as good as the father, which would be sad for the son. Or they might say that the father was not as good as the son, which would be sad for the father. But if one wrote and the other drew, they could each happily tell themselves that they were both equally clever.

So from time to time I was given pencil, paper and a profile and set to work. The result was then slipped into the wallet to be produced later at the Garrick. "Oh, by the way, you might like to see what my boy did yesterday." Or: "I think I might have something of his in my pocket. Not too bad really, considering he has never had any lessons." And then the question of possible lessons might follow. Perhaps Munnings could give some advice. (He didn't, but he gave me a signed print of one of his paintings.) Perhaps George Morrow might come round one day. (He said he might but he never did, and we made the obvious joke as we waited hopefully.) Anyway, lessons or no lessons – and it was beginning to look a little like no lessons – it was an enjoyable way of spending an evening.

And here I am, at the age of about eight, settling down to enjoy it. First, the bulging forehead, where all those brains were. Would I have a bulging forehead like that one day? I hoped so. Eating fish was supposed to help. I must eat lots of fish. I liked cods' roe and haddock. . . . Then the nose, large, beaky and easy. Noses were easy in profile, not so easy if they came straight at you. . . . Now the mouth. "I'm doing your mouth. Could you possibly take your pipe out just for a moment?" The mouth always went wrong and had to be rubbed out several times. It always came too heavy. My father had a thin, delicate mouth, and a lot of the sort of person he was could be seen in it. So if you got it wrong you had drawn someone quite different. . . . "Done it, but it's not very good. You can go on smoking now." . . . The chin was a lot easier, and so was the neck with its large Adam's apple. . . . And that finished the right-hand side. Now for some bits in the middle. The eye first. The eye was even harder than the mouth. There was so little to it, yet so much of my father was in his eyes. They were blue and like the blue sea they could be warm and caressing or icy cold. Mostly they were warm and kind and gentle and humorous and perhaps a little mocking but always understanding. But how did you get all this into a few pencil lines? . . . I sighed and went on to the ear which, though full of intricate loops and curls, was easy once you were sure you were putting it in the right place. . . . Then the thin fair hair brushed back to cover the bald spot. . . . A few final touches: the curly line joining nostril to corner of mouth, the pipe to disguise some of the smudges round the mouth, back of head, collar, tie. . . . "Done it!" I passed it over. My father studied it. "It's not bad," he said. "Not at all bad." He tried covering the lower half with his hand, then the upper half. Was the top half better than the bottom or the bottom better than the top? The eye wasn't quite right; the mouth a little odd. But the nose was quite good. It *was* hard to get a likeness. How did one do it? Perhaps George Morrow, if he ever came, would tell us. . . .

Well, if I failed, at least I failed in good company. Others tried – distinguished professionals – and they did no better. Only Spy in his full length portrait really – triumphantly – succeeded. What was it about my father that made him so hard to draw? And why, when he was so hard to draw, was he so easy to photograph?

Not long ago I came upon a photograph of my father taken when he was about 18 years old and showing him with his brothers, Barry and Ken. I had not seen a photograph of my father as a young man before; and as for my uncles, I had no idea at all what they looked like, either then or at any other time; for I never met them. I wouldn't have met Barry: my father never even spoke of him. And Ken had died when I was eight. I knew my aunts Connie and Maud well enough and I knew my cousins; but of my uncles I knew only what my father's autobiography told me: that he had disliked Barry (though it was never made clear exactly why), and that – for reasons all too obvious – he had adored Ken. And now, seventy years after it had been taken, here was this photograph of the three of them. It was, in its small, private way, a dramatic meeting. It would have been that in any case, however indifferent the photograph. But the photograph was very far from being indifferent. It was eloquent beyond anything I had ever seen. It was not content to show me three young men. It told me all about them.

In a single snapshot everything that I knew about the three brothers was confirmed and much that I didn't know became clear. There in the middle is brother Barry. But can he really be their brother? Is he really a Milne? He looks so different. Everything about him is different from the other two. His hair is black and curly and parted in the middle. Theirs is fair and straight and parted on the side. Ken and Alan are dressed alike in dark suits and stiff white collars. Barry is wearing a Norfolk jacket and knickerbockers. And since there is only one chair, it is of course Barry who is sitting in it, leaving the others to stand on either side. They are clearly posing for their photograph, thinking it all a bit of a lark. "All right then, here we are, the three Milnes. Fire away and don't blame us if it breaks the camera." And you can see at a glance that Barry is Mephistopheles and that inside himself he is chuckling "Ho, ho, ho!" And Ken is St. George and inside himself he is laughing "Ha, ha, ha!" You feel you know both Barry and Ken and that if you were an artist your fingers would itch to put it all down on paper. But Alan? Alan is different. Alan is difficult. He is clearly Ken's man, dressed like Ken, looking like Ken, on Ken's side and so on the side of the angels. But Alan doesn't wear his heart on his sleeve as the others do. Alan's heart is firmly buttoned up inside his jacket and only the merest hint of it can be seen dancing in his eyes, flickering in the corners of his mouth. You can see now why Alan has always been so difficult to draw.

Difficult to draw, yet easy to photograph. Artists failed. Photographers – even unskilled amateur photographers – succeeded. What about writers? What about an unskilled amateur writer? Well, I must just do my best. Luckily I shan't be attempting anything too ambitious, certainly not a full length study, just a collection of snapshots.

My father's heart remained buttoned up all through his life, and I wouldn't want now to attempt to unbutton it, to write about the things he never spoke about. All I hope to do is to catch some of the overflow that came bubbling out and get it on to the page before it runs to waste. No more than that.

CHAPTER 16
She Laughed at My Jokes

Alan Milne married Dorothy de Selincourt in 1913. This, of course, was before my time, and since they didn't talk to me about those early days (why should they?), I have to rely now on my father's autobiography for information. Not that he gives much. However, two sentences are all I need for the present. The first is: "She laughed at my jokes."

Surely this is the one absolutely vital qualification for a professional humorist's wife: that she should laugh at his jokes. Jokes are delicate things and my father's were especially delicate. Was it funny? Only someone's laughter would tell you. Only someone's laughter would encourage you to go on trying to be funny. It is true that a writer writes first to please himself and that his own satisfaction with what he has done is perhaps his greatest satisfaction. But writing is a means of communication. It is not enough to speak; you must also be heard. The message must be received and understood. Also a writer needs praise. At least my father did. He needed someone to say: "I loved it, darling. It was awfully good." Of course, anyone who is well trained can say that without really meaning it, and I know that on one or two rare occasions my mother did.

You can pretend to admire, but, unless you are a superb actress, you can't pretend to laugh. Laughter is genuine or else it is just a noise.

So if a marriage bureau had been trying to fit my father with a suitable partner, a girl who laughed at his jokes, who shared his sense of humour, would be at the top of the list quite regardless of any other qualifications. Did it matter that she couldn't play golf? Did it matter that she didn't enjoy watching cricket? Did it matter that she wasn't very brainy? Not in the least.

Of course, young married couples like doing things together, delight in sharing each other's pleasures. So perhaps in those early days there were moments of sadness, as when my mother discovered that my father didn't like rice pudding, or when my father had to admit that my mother would never be any good with a mashie-niblick. In fact, there were really very few things that they did enjoy doing together. So wisely, they did them separately, then met afterwards and told each other of their adventures: and if something funny had happened to one of them, they could laugh together about it and be happy.

This meant that when, in 1930, I came downstairs to join them, I found that I was either doing things with my mother or doing things with my father; not very often with both. It all seemed quite natural. I wasn't expecting my mother to bowl to me at our net in the meadow, or come looking for birds' nests. And if she and I were engaged on some sort of redecoration in the house or work in the garden, I wasn't expecting more than just admiration from my father when it was done. So far as I know, both my mother and my father continued to enjoy in married life all the pleasures they had enjoyed when single. They had been enjoying them alone. Now they could enjoy them with me.

No. This is not quite true. There is one possible exception, one pleasure that I think my mother had to sacrifice.

This is guesswork on my part. For she never admitted it.

Indeed she may never have been consciously aware of it. My clue is a remark she made. It struck me as surprising at the time and so I remembered it. And now, sorting through my jumble of memories, I have come upon it with its label "Surprising Remark" and the date: 1940.

We were at Cotchford. We had left London for good, but my father had gone up for the day, as he did once a week, and I was alone with my mother. It was not a very nice day, not nice enough to be out of doors, and there was nothing special I wanted to do indoors. So I thought I would listen to a concert on the wireless. This was a thing I had never done at home before. We had a wireless but didn't use it for music – just for the news and perhaps also the Saturday night play (which my mother enjoyed up to the point at which she fell asleep and which my father and I were more or less able to read our books through). It was a pity about music, a pity good music meant so little to either of them, not that our wireless was really much use if you wanted to listen to that sort of thing: for it had been chosen for its smallness and neatness and elegance, not for its voice. However, it was better than nothing. I was rather hoping that my mother was going to be upstairs in her bedroom, but she had come down and was now lying on one of the sofas reading. Bother! But it couldn't be helped. I took the wireless to the other sofa at the other end of the room by the window and turned it on not too loud. I loved music. I had discovered my love for it at school when I had discovered that I could sing. Since I can't sing at all now, and since I can look back on my boyhood self as someone quite different from me today, I feel that it is not being boastful if I say that I used to be able to sing very well indeed. The music cup at Boxgrove bore my name for three successive years. In fact my father was so impressed by my voice that he bought me a ukelele and had someone in to teach me to play it. "It's only a shanty in old shanty town," I crooned to him, "The roof is so slanty it touches the ground". When the music master at Stowe, searching for talent among the new boys, had shaken my top A out of his ears, he asked me if I also played any instrument. "A ukelele," I said proudly. "I don't call that an instrument," he answered. Nor, now, do I, but I was a bit hurt at the time. I wish now that I had learned to play something – some proper instrument – to replace the voice I lost when, a year later, it broke. But there it was, and I could at least enjoy listening. I had a gramophone at school. My parents had given it to me. They had chosen it for its neatness and elegance; but luckily my study companion had one too, and his had been chosen for its voice. So we listened to Sibelius on his.

And now I was listening to Elgar's violin concerto, and when it was over I turned the wireless off. I had been playing it quite softly. I hoped I hadn't disturbed my mother. She had been very quiet, perhaps reading, perhaps sleeping. And now came her remark: "I liked that," she said.

When my father made Rabbit say to Owl: "You and I have brains. The others have fluff", he might have been thinking of the de Selincourts. For there was no doubt that Uncle Ernest, the famous Wordsworth scholar, had immense brain, and so had brother Aubrey. And there is equally little doubt that Dorothy and brother Bob had fluff. But if there had been this unequal distribution of brain among the family, all, in their individual ways, were artistic. This turned the brainy ones into intellectuals, making them, in the eyes of the unbrainy, totally unbearable. They talked about Art in a solemn and learned manner which the others couldn't stand. One can imagine Uncle Ernest sweeping Aubrey off to the Tate Gallery or the Queen's Hall, leaving Dorothy, to whom "*chiaroscuro*" and "*allegro vivace*" meant absolutely nothing at all, upstairs in her bedroom, contemplating her wardrobe and humming her own private home-made hums. If only Beethoven didn't have to be surrounded by all this eyes-shut, lips-pursed stuff, this intenseness, this awful Uncle Ernest, she might have enjoyed him.

Then came Alan. And now comes my second quotation from

his autobiography: ". . . and I, in my turn, had a pianola to which she was devoted, and from which I could not keep her away."

Go on: smile. You are meant to. It is a little joke. You don't really imagine girls can be devoted to pianolas, surely!

Alan was brainy, but Alan was not artistic. And so Alan mercifully was not intellectual. He disliked Uncle Ernest as much as did Dorothy. If Alan knew Tennyson by heart, this only meant that he could be relied on to do the Tennyson quotations in *The Times* crossword. Alan and Dorothy, as well as laughing at the same jokes, would laugh together at intellectuals. But, alas, Alan was not musical. The pianola led nowhere. Poor Dorothy! She could read her own books. She could decorate her bedroom to her own taste. There were many things which she could do on her own, but listening to music was not among them: this was something that they had to do together. Together they enjoyed Sullivan and Jerome Kern. Together they went to *Stop Flirting, No, No, Nanette* and *Music in the Air*. And if, on the following day, my father said: "That was a catchy little song at the end of the second Act. How did it go?", my mother would think a little, then try out a few notes, stop, shake her head, look up at the ceiling, smile, try again – nearly – once more – Got it! And she would be off, humming it all, perfectly remembered. She liked what she liked: that was something. But she might have liked so much more.

Sullivan, of course, was also Gilbert. Musical comedy was comedy as well as music. And so, sitting side by side in the stalls, listening to the music, they could also laugh at the words. And so, too, could I. And since so much of the holidays was going to be spent doing things either with my mother or with my father, how nice to start with something we could all three enjoy together. What shall it be this time? Hooray! Leslie Henson, Fred Emney and Richard Hearne were on at the Gaiety. This was my absolute favourite. Or perhaps it might be

Bobby Howes. Or Arthur Riscoe. Once it was Jack Hulbert and Cicely Courtneidge, and I enjoyed myself so much that in the interval a box of chocolates was brought round for me. "For *me*?" "Yes, sir. It is from Miss Courtneidge. She said it was for the little boy who is laughing so loudly."

So you see, whether you are an actress or whether you are a writer, it is all the same. You *do* need someone to laugh at your jokes.

CHAPTER 17

Green Sweets

Today we "do-it-ourselves". Indeed we do so much ourselves that it is hard to remember there was a time, not so very long ago, when a newly-married couple could manage virtually nothing without help. Naturally they couldn't tackle the wall papering or fix the leaky tap: even today we feel quite proud of ourselves if we can cope with that. But neither could they sweep the floor or make the beds or do the laundry. Nor could they cook or wash up. At least they couldn't if one of them was a de Selincourt. Dorothy had never been taught any of these things. From time to time my father and I used to wonder just what it was that Dorothy *had* been taught. We knew that she had been "finished" in France. But where and with what it had all begun remained a mystery.

Dorothy was not brainy. No one expected her to shine at algebra. But this still left plenty of things that she could have learnt and which she would have enjoyed doing and done well if only this had been proper. In the 1914–18 war when it was all right for nicely brought up young ladies to do manual work for the sake of our gallant boys, my mother had learnt to tie up parcels. I'm not sure what went inside them, probably comforts

5a. Galleons Lap: drawing by E. H. Shepard

5b. Gill's Lap today

6a. Christopher

6b. Christopher Robin as Shepard
saw him

for the troops, Balaclava helmets and socks lovingly knitted by other young ladies. This was, almost certainly, the only practical thing she was ever properly taught how to do in her whole life, and the result was that she did it both then and ever afterwards exceedingly well. If today I am an expert parcel tier myself – and I may say that I am an expert parcel tier – it is because I learnt the craft at my mother's knee. I used to watch her fascinated: the brisk competent folding of the paper that pressed the misshapen contents into a neat, firm rectangular form; the string tied so quickly, so tightly and with such an economy of knots; the result so solid and symmetrical that it seemed wrong that anyone should ever want to open it. Today from time to time I try to pass on this skill to others, but I know that, however hard I try, all they will be able to manage in the end is a squashy brown bundle loosely slung in a hammock of string. Pick it up at the wrong end, give it a shake, and all has to be done again.

But if my mother was taught to tie up parcels, she was (naturally) never taught to untie them. She was at the supplying end, not the receiving end. And anyway undoing parcels was not really a thing that needed lessons. So she taught herself. She did it by the light of nature. She merely reversed the process of tying up. It took about half an hour if the knots were tight. It left my father and myself jumping up and down with impatience if the parcel was an exciting one. "Oh, go on. *Cut* it!" But no. String was precious. You can't buy string. At least my mother wouldn't have known how to set about trying to buy it. And you can't buy paper. So it all had to be saved. "Anyway, I like undoing parcels," she said as she wound up the string on her hand. "Don't rush me," she said as she carefully flattened the crumples out of the paper.

My mother was practical. She was no good at games. Give her a putter and you only had to see the way she held it to realize that. But just watch her with a pair of shears cutting the grass! I still model my technique on hers. My father was the reverse, a natural games player, at his happiest with a club or a bat, but all fumbles with any sort of tool. "You're not exactly the neat-handed Phyllis," as my mother once pointed out to him.

My mother would have made a good cook. But young ladies weren't taught cooking. They were not taught gardening either; but there is a difference between the two. No matter how many gardeners there are, it is still possible for the mistress to have her own trowel and her own pair of secateurs. There are still things that the mistress can do and do well and which the gardener will be only too happy to let her do. But in the kitchen there can only be one cook. So if you've never been told how to boil an egg or make a pot of tea, and if the presence of cook makes experiment impossible, you will go through life without ever knowing. My mother never knew. She visited the kitchen from time to time. In London she visited it every morning and spent half an hour or so with Mrs. Gulliver planning menus and chatting about this and that. At Cotchford the menus were left to Mrs. Wilson and her visits were less frequent. But I doubt if she ever watched the experts at their work. I remember an occasion after the war when I was visiting Cotchford for a weekend. Things were a little different now. Times had changed. There was an awareness of the fact that Mrs. Wilson wasn't getting any younger, that the presence of visitors made extra work for her, and that we must all do our bit to help. So after tea the tray was carried into the hall; then, one by one, the cups and plates and saucers were taken into the little washroom (where in the old days the pumping used to be done). And I can see my mother now, plate held under the tap, forefinger delicately urging fragments of jam towards the drain. "I always think," she said, "that getting jam off plates must be the hardest part of washing up."

The reader may smile at this naïveté, may think how lucky people were in those days to have cooks to cook and maids to wash and scrub. And indeed an author today, who, when not writing, is probably bathing the baby or making the breakfast or washing up the supper or hoovering the hall or any one of a hundred domestic chores, may well envy my father who wrote from about 10.30 in the morning until just before lunch and from after tea until just before dinner, and who could then do just as he pleased for the whole of the rest of the day. Nevertheless, there is another side to it, which I must mention.

If, for instance, you boil your own egg and give it four minutes and it is too soft, the matter is easily remedied: next time you give it five minutes. But if the egg has been cooked by cook and brought in by the maid and is then discovered to be too soft, the problem is virtually insoluble.

"Oh, dear. My egg's all runny."

"Don't you like it like that?"

"Well, you know I don't. I don't mind the yolk a bit soft but I don't like being able to see it through the white."

"What a fuss-pot you are."

"I'd rather it was too hard than too soft. You couldn't mention it to Mrs. Wilson, perhaps."

"But you've been having eggs like this for years. I can't suddenly say you don't like them. She'd be terribly upset."

However good they are – and both Mrs. Wilson and Mrs. Gulliver were very good – cooks do bring a certain inflexibility to the menu. Eggs, once soft-boiled, remain soft-boiled for ever. It was much the same with coffee. We had coffee after dinner at Mallord Street. Why did we never have it at Cotchford? Just because we never did: the opportunity for asking for it had been missed and now it was too late. Anyway, there would be coffee again when we got back to London, "And it's nice not always having everything the same," said my mother. But when we left London for good in 1940 we were faced with coffeeless evenings for the rest of our lives unless something was done about it; and somewhere around seven years later the innovation was achieved. Great excitement. Great congratulations. A landmark in our lives. My father ladled in the sugar, stirred and drank, paused, drank again, then looked across at my mother.

"Do you think she's got it quite right?"

"Why, what's the matter?"

"Well, mine tastes salty. She can't have muddled up the salt with the sugar, can she?"

"You're supposed to put a little salt in. She told me so. It brings out the flavour."

My father took another sip

"Darling, this is really quite undrinkable."

"Oh, it's not as bad as all that. You can't leave it. She'd be so hurt."

So we used to drink it. It was frightful and we drank it very fast, like medicine.

But if the great coffee innovation was a failure, there were others that were more successful. There was, for instance, the occasion when my mother and I decided that as we didn't like tea for breakfast there was really no reason why we should always have to drink it. We could drink something else instead. Brilliant idea! So I chose Horlicks and enjoyed my breakfasts much more. Then there were the fish paste sandwiches, wafer-thin crustless triangles, that we always had at tea time. I think my father was supposed to like them, and perhaps he did. But did I? One day, after I had been eating them for about five years, the question was asked. No as a matter of fact, I didn't. I'd much rather have a nice thick crust of bread and perhaps a tomato. "And I don't see why you shouldn't, you poor little thing," said my mother. So from then on that's what I had, and tea joined breakfast as another meal to look forward to.

Now just as naturalists learn a lot about the creatures they are studying by observing their eating habits, so can we, by watching them at their dinner table, learn at lot about human beings. But it is not enough to know what they like; one must also discover what they dislike. And this as I have shown is made very much easier if there is a professional cook on the premises.

Here are some more things that the observer, lurking in the shadows of our dining-room, might have noted. My father put six lumps of sugar into his tea, but he disliked chocolate soufflé and instead was served with his own small cheese soufflé. With my mother it was the other way about: no sugar in her tea but a passion for rich puddings. My father liked milk but not milk puddings, my mother milk puddings but not milk. A study of what they ate might then be followed by a study of how they ate and again certain differences would be noticed. Knives and forks being tools, it is perhaps not surprising that my mother handled hers with great dexterity, my father with his usual clumsiness. (It was generally agreed within the family that my father couldn't eat a pear without getting his elbows wet, and that after a honey sandwich he had to have a bath.) I said in a previous chapter that there was something cat-like about my mother. There was something cat-like about the way she ate, too. Just as a cat will lick at a saucer on and on until not even the ghost of a smell remains, so would my mother scrape at her plate, not greedily, just methodically, until it was spotless. My father, on the other hand, mushed his food up and then left all the bits he didn't like – the gristly bits, the stringy bits, the skinny bits – round the edge. And because they were so different, each found the other's habits mildly irritating. "I wonder why you always have to mash up your strawberries in that rather repellent way."

What conclusions, I wonder, would the observer draw from all this. He would spot that my mother ate omnivorously and elegantly and that my father ate fussily and messily. But would he notice that my father also ate nostalgically? Probably not, though he might have listed some odd likes and dislikes that seemed without obvious explanation.

Why, for example, did my father, who disliked every other form of milk pudding, have such a passion for crème brulée? What was there so very special about "ham-and-eggs"? Why, with his sweet tooth, did he not share my mother's Charbonnel et Walker chocolates but prefer his own private acid drops? And finally, what was the origin of the mystique that surrounded the Green Sweets?

The answer to all these questions is that my father ate not just for present pleasure but also to re-evoke past pleasures. In the way that smells are nostalgic to most of us, so to him were tastes. Crème brulée he loved because it reminded him of when and where he had so happily first discovered it – as an undergraduate at Cambridge. "Ham-and-eggs" was what he and Ken restored themselves with on their numerous walking and bicycling expeditions. "We then had a lovely dinner of ham and eggs ... We had a tremendous tea of ham and eggs ..." wrote my father in his school magazine. This particular walk was nineteen miles and Alan was only $8\frac{1}{2}$ years old; so his hunger can be understood. And so, too, his thirst. "We went into a shop and bought some ginger beer ... When we got there we bought some biscuits and some ginger beer ..." Ham and eggs and ginger beer, this was what the two wayfarers invariably asked for when they stopped for refreshment. Forty years later my father was once again asking for it when he and I were on the road. Did the ginger beer still taste as good as in those golden childhood days? Did it matter if it didn't?

As for acid drops, he didn't in fact particularly like them, just liked having them. They were his "suckers", and his time for eating them – if at all – was when my mother and I had gone up to bed and he was alone. Did he and Ken spend their pocket money on suckers? They certainly wouldn't have been able to afford Charbonnel et Walker. Unlike Dorothy, they were not rich. They enjoyed modest pleasures; and it was these modest pleasures that my father from time to time loved to return to. "Ham-and-eggs" at an inn, ginger beer in a pub, acid drops in a paper bag. It was exciting to dine in style at The Ivy but not so memorable (because memory-recalling) as the meal the two of us sometimes had towards the end of the winter holidays. "Let's go to an ABC for lunch." "Oh, do let's." My mother was going to be out, lunching with a friend. We would be alone together. It was our chance. . . . There was an ABC at the far end of the King's Road just before you got to Sloane Square. That was the one we went to, and we went there by bus, of course, for the bus trip was part of the memory. My father had scrambled eggs on toast (they didn't run to "ham-and-eggs") and I had baked beans on toast. And when the holidays were over and I was back at school, his first letter to me would recall that happy lunch that he and I had had to-gether. He and I – and the ghost of Ken. . . .

There are some secrets that we long to solve. We are in-trigued by the problem and long to know the answer. But there are others that are best left as they are: where an aura of mystery is worth more than the probably rather prosaic solution. In such a category I put the Green Sweets. They were a sort of crème de menthe Turkish delight, round and flat like a peppermint cream, and they were called "Starboard Lights". They lived in their own special amber cut-glass jars on the dining-room table; and after lunch and after dinner we each had one – just one: never two. It was a sort of ritual. During the war these very special sweets became hard to find. "I'm afraid this is the best Mrs. Wilson could manage". "But they're terrible, not right at all, much too gummy." So friends in London were told to keep a look-out. "They must be 'Starboard Lights': nothing else will do"; and sometimes a tin was discovered, and, oh, what joy it brought. . . . Where, I wonder, did it all start? What memories were recalled twice a day every day, year after year? When at last it all came to an end – Mallord Street sold, Cotchford sold, all the family treasures dispersed – one thing only I kept as a reminder: the pair of jars that had housed the Green Sweets since before I was born. Somewhere inside them was locked away the secret of the happiness they gave. I shall never discover it. I don't want to learn it. It is enough to look at them from time to time and know that it is there.

CHAPTER 18
The Enthusiast

Grandfather Milne was a schoolmaster. To be specific, Grandfather Milne was the headmaster of a boys' private school called Henley House. Among his more distinguished assistant masters he could count H. G. Wells and among his more distinguished pupils his two sons, Ken and Alan.

Of Alan he once wrote, in the school magazine:

He does not like French – does not see that you prove anything when you have done. Thinks mathematics grand. He leaves his books about; loses his pen; can't imagine what he did with this, and where he put that, but is convinced that it is somewhere. Clears his brain when asked a question by spurting out some nonsense, and then immediately after gives a sensible reply. Can speak 556 words per minute, and writes more in three minutes than his instructor can read in thirty. Finds this a very interesting world, and would like to learn physiology, botany, geology, astronomy and everything else. Wishes to make a collection of beetles, bones, butterflies, etc., and cannot determine whether Algebra is better than football or Euclid than a sponge cake.[1]

[1] Quoted in *It's Too Late Now*.

As my father commented: "It is the portrait of an enthusiast."

Being one of the brightest pupils of a very good headmaster and at the same time the fond son of a loving parent gave my father an attitude towards schools and teaching not generally shared by other parents. He was once the guest at a dinner party of Preparatory Schoolmasters:

They all, so it seemed, made speeches; two Public School Headmasters made speeches; and the burden of all their speeches was the obstructiveness of the Parent to their beneficent labours. I had disclaimed any desire to make a speech, but by this time I wanted to. That very evening, offered the alternatives of a proposition of Euclid's or a chapter of *Treasure Island* as a bedtime story, my own boy had chosen Euclid: it was "so much more fun". All children, I said (perhaps rashly) are like that. There is nothing that they are not eager to learn. "And then we send them to your schools, and in two years, three years, four years, you have killed all their enthusiasm. At fifteen their only eagerness is to escape learning anything. No wonder you don't want to meet us."[1]

My father knew a good schoolmaster from a bad one. He set high standards, and felt that he was in a position – both as the son of a headmaster and the father of a pupil whose bills he was paying – to make criticisms. Even in the best schools lapses could occur, mistakes could be made, and these must be put right. One day I came home from Gibbs and told him that we had been learning all about the Georges. "George I 1714 to 1727, George II 1727 to 1759, George III 1759 to . . ." "1759?" said my father. "Are you sure?" "Quite sure. That's what Miss McSheehy said." "Not 1760?" "No." We were in his library, the dark room at the back of the house in Mallord Street where he wrote. All the way round, from floor to ceiling, were bookshelves. Somewhere here, surely, he would

[1] *It's Too Late Now.*

find confirmation. . . . He went across, looked, then took out a book and opened it. "I thought so. George II 1727 to 1760. We'd better put them right on that." And so he did. That evening he rang up Mr. Gibbs. Next morning in class we chanted our knowledge: "George I 1714 to 1727. George II 1727 to . . ." "One moment, please." Miss McSheehy held up her hand. Then with a smile she pointed at me. "You tell them, Christopher." "1727 to 1760", I said rather smugly. Uproar. Indignation. Cries of "No!" and "But you told us . . ." And Miss McSheehy smiling through it all. She was a good and dedicated teacher. Accuracy was what mattered. Anyway the fault had not really been hers. It was in the book she had been using. She had shown it to Mr. Gibbs and he had quoted it to my father. "I have it before me in black and white," he had said. But then he had referred to other books, and they had said differently. . . .

But if my father could stand up to schoolmasters and if he inherited some of his own father's gifts as a teacher, he himself could never have become one. He could teach and loved teaching. He could radiate enthusiasm, but he could never impose discipline. He could never have taught a dull subject to a dull boy, never have said: "Do this because I say so." Enthusiasm spread knowledge sideways, among equals. Discipline forced it downwards from above. My father's relationships were always between equals, however old or young, distinguished or undistinguished the other person. Once, when I was quite little, he came up to the nursery while I was having my lunch. And while he was talking I paused between mouthfuls, resting my hands on the table, knife and fork pointing upwards. "You oughtn't really to sit like that," he said, gently. "Why not?" I asked, surprised. "Well . . ." He hunted around for a reason he could give. Because it's considered bad manners? Because you mustn't? Because . . . "Well," he said, looking in the direction that my fork was pointing, "Suppose somebody suddenly fell through the ceiling. They might land on your fork and that would be very painful." "I see," I said, though I didn't really. It seemed such an unlikely thing to happen, such a funny reason for holding your knife and fork flat when you were not using them. . . . But funny reason or not, it seems I have remembered it. In the same sort of way I learned about the nesting habits of starlings. I had been given a bird book for Easter (Easter 1934: I have the book still) and with its help I had made my first discovery. "There's a blackbird's nest in the hole under the tiles just outside the drawing-room window," I announced proudly. "I've just seen the blackbird fly in". "I think it's probably really a starling," said my father. "No, it's a blackbird," I said firmly, hating to be wrong, hating being corrected. "Well," said my father, realizing how I felt but at the same time unable to allow an inaccuracy to get away with it, "Perhaps it's a blackbird visiting a starling." A blackbird visiting a starling. Someone falling through the ceiling. He could never bear to be dogmatic, never bring himself to say (in effect): This is so because I say it is, and I am older than you and must know better. How much easier, how much nicer to escape into the world of fantasy in which he felt himself so happily at home.

Luckily for him, I was, as he had been, an enthusiastic learner, eager to sit beside him on the sofa and be shown how one solved simultaneous equations. It is true that mathematics didn't lead anywhere, neither in his day nor in mine. It had got him a scholarship to Westminster and an exhibition to Trinity College, Cambridge. It got me a scholarship to Harrow (by mistake) and another to Stowe (which was what I really wanted) and then, later, one to Trinity. But after that, with both of us, our enthusiasm burnt itself out. The exciting road we had been following had come to an end: almost the only prospect open to the mathematician was to become a mathematics master; and neither of us could have faced that.

So as we sat side by side, it was not of my future career that my father was thinking, but of the immediate present. For now, at long last, Nanny was out of the way. Now at last he and I could do things together. Here after ten years of waiting was his opportunity to share with me his boyhood enthusiasms, to relive his own boyhood through me, and in the process to find my love.

How long would it last? How long does a son feel for his father that very special love that he knew so well? With him it had lasted until he was twelve but with him it had started so very much earlier. Would I stay with him a little longer to make up for those lost years? Till fourteen, perhaps, or sixteen? He was lucky. We were together until I was eighteen, very, very close. He knew he was lucky, that he had got perhaps more than he deserved, and he was very grateful. And once, a little shyly, he thanked me. . . .

Father and son. What sort of relationship is it? Does the father look down to the son, the son look up to the father? Or does the father get on to his hands and knees so that they are both on the same level? Sometimes the one, sometimes the other; but in our case neither would do. We had to be on the same level, but we both had to be standing, for my father couldn't bend, couldn't pretend to be what he wasn't. We could do algebra together, and Euclid, and look for birds' nests, and catch things in the stream, and play cricket in the meadow. We could putt on the lawn and throw tennis balls at each other. We could do those things as equals. But what about those other moments, which adults pass in casual chit-chat, which husband and wife can so happily share in complete silence content to be in each other's company? Meal times. Car journeys. After dinner in front of the fire. Conversation with a small child is difficult. Perhaps instead one might learn the morse code. My father had learnt it during the war when he was battalion signals officer. So now he taught me and with hand squeezes we were able to pass messages to each other as Burnside drove us down to Cotchford. Then at lunch time mightn't I feel a bit left out if he and my mother discussed dull, grown-up things? So, "How about a game?" he would say, and we would play clumps, or go through the alphabet to see how many flowers we could name beginning with each letter in turn. And finally, after dinner, almost a ritual, there was *The Times* crossword, with my mother (to give her a slight advantage) reading out the clues and my father trying not to be too quick with the answers.

My father had a passion for crosswords. We shared the *Times*: this was the rule. It was fairly easy. It took about half an hour, and though he would get most of the answers (including all the quotations), my mother and I would be able to manage a few contributions. On Sunday we took the *Observer* and so on Sunday evening we did the "Everyman" crossword. This left my father free to wrestle single-handed with his favourite Torquemada.

How many Torquemada solvers survive today? Any that do will surely agree that his were the most difficult crosswords and he the most brilliant composer of them all; and that even Ximenes, good though he was, was never quite in the same class.

Solving crosswords is immensely satisfying. In a way it is the same sort of satisfaction you get from solving mathematical problems. Pencil, paper and brains: that's what you need. And you wrestle away until at last the answer comes. Or you can describe it as fitting words into an exact, interlocking pattern of squares. You can't alter the pattern: that is fixed. You juggle with the words, juggle with the letters, until at last it all fits, until the last letter falls neatly, satisfyingly into place. "Got it!" and with a happy sigh you put your pencil back in your pocket. In this respect it resembles the writing of light verse. Does this sound surprising? Then I must get my father to explain.

Charles Stuart Calverley was born on December 17th, 1831. He was the supreme master of one of the loveliest of arts:

an art, even at its most popular, practised by few and appreciated by not many more: now a dying art, having such exigent laws, and making such demands on the craftsmanship of its practitioners, that it has no place in a brave, new, unperspiring world: the Art of Light Verse. I propose to be so old-fashioned as to write in praise of it.

Light Verse obeys Coleridge's definition of poetry, the best words in the best order; it demands Carlyle's definition of genius, transcendent capacity for taking pains; and it is the supreme exhibition of somebody's definition of art, the concealment of art. In the result it observes the most exact laws of rhyme and metre as if by happy accident, and in a sort of nonchalant spirit of mockery at the real poets who do it on purpose. But to describe it so leaves something unsaid; one must say what it is not. Light Verse, then, is not the relaxation of a major poet in the intervals of writing an epic. . . . It is a precise art which has only been taken seriously, and thus qualified as an art, in the nineteenth and twentieth centuries. . . . Light Verse is not the output of poets at play, but of light-verse writers at the hardest and most severely technical work known to authorship.[1]

Light verse started where almost everything else in my father's life started – with Ken. They were young men, Alan still at home, Ken articled to a solicitor, when they made the unexpected discovery that each had a talent for it. "Good Heavens," wrote Ken in answer to Alan's first effort, "You can do it too." So from then on they collaborated, and for two years they wrote light verse together.

"Writing light verse in collaboration is easier than one would think," wrote my father.

I don't mean by "easy" what our fellow Westminster, Cowper, meant when he boasted of the ease with which he wrote *John Gilpin*. . . . What I mean is that light verse offers

[1] *Year in, Year out*, published in 1952.

more scope for collaboration than at first thought seems possible. For a set of light verses, like a scene of stage dialogue, is never finished. One can go on and on and on, searching for the better word, the more natural phrase. There comes a time when one is in danger of losing all sense of values, and then one's collaborator steps in suddenly with what one sees at once is the perfect word.[1]

But this is only true if the two collaborators are at the same level, as Ken and Alan were when they started. If one is a professional and the other only a beginner, the beginner has little he can contribute. So he and I did not collaborate as he and Ken had done. There were verses in his letters to me. There were, rather more rarely, verses in my letters to him. But there were no verses that were the joint work of the two of us. . . . You can't teach someone how to write light verse. You can tell him the rules, your rules, the rules of your generation. But even the rules may change . . .

In my day (wrote my father) poets said what they had to say in song. This song (poetry it was called) demanded rhyme or, at least, rhythm from its devotees, and in consequence was hard work. It was obvious, therefore, that if you were going to improve poetry you would improve it most comfortably by omitting the things which were difficult to manage – rhyme and rhythm – and concentrating on what might come to anybody, inspiration.[1]

There was anyway not much point in teaching a dying art. Better stick to mathematics. After all, mathematics was where it had all started with him. Mathematics had led to light verse, to articles in *Punch*, to plays, to Pooh. Mathematics could in the same way start me off on the road to wherever it was I was going.

Where *was* I going? "The boy, what will he become?"

[1] *It's Too Late Now*.

How easy if my father had been a publisher instead of an author; for then I could have entered the family business and taken over from him when he retired. But an author has nothing tangible that he can hand on to his son. Only a handful of talents. A mathematical brain, perhaps, a sense of humour, an aptitude for games. Where did that lead you? Perhaps it didn't really matter. Perhaps it didn't matter what you did in life provided you did it as well as you were able to and provided you did it happily.

These, really, were his two great talents: perfectionism and enthusiasm. He handed them on to me – and he could have given me nothing more precious.

7. A. A. Milne and Christopher Milne

8. A. A. Milne: cartoon by Spy

CHAPTER 19

Eeyore's Gloomy Place

Where did Eeyore live? The others lived on the Forest or in the Hundred Acre Wood. But where was the Gloomy Place? If I were pressed I would say that the actual gloomy place was the bottom corner of the field where we used to keep Jessica. It was a very wild, tussocky, thistly field and the bottom corner was suitably marshy. With a donkey living there anyway (though not a specially gloomy one: moody, rather) this would seem the obvious spot. Yet I don't feel quite happy about it, and I think the reason is that elsewhere it was fact that inspired fiction – Gills Lap that inspired Galleon's Lap, the group of pine trees on the other side of the main road that became the Six Pine Trees, the bridge over the river at Posingford that became Pooh-sticks Bridge. But here it was the other way round. So that if there was an original Gloomy Place before Eeyore came along to take possession of it, it was not here. Perhaps it was nowhere. Or perhaps . . .

Mallord Street was my mother's work: hers alone. My father paid the bills but it was she who planned it all – who chose the furniture and the carpets and the curtains and the colour of the walls – she who decided what (and indeed who) would go where. But if there was no collaboration, there was also no argument. It was agreed that the house was her domain, and that, provided she didn't spend money that wasn't there, she could rule as she pleased. And this she did. She was a firm ruler. If there were any obstacles in the way she would ignore them. If any unwelcome facts upset her hopes, she would treat them as if they didn't exist. I suggested earlier that one of the unwelcome facts that faced her soon after my arrival was that I was clearly a boy, and that for nine years she tried to ignore this by dressing me as a girl. I am not entirely sure how seriously I take this theory, but at least it is not out of character. Fortunately, in this particular instance, mind failed to triumph over matter and I remained a boy. But only just; and I was one of her few failures.

But if she was an autocrat, she was a benevolent autocrat. She ruled well; and the house, and all who visited it, all who lived in it, all who worked in it, would pay unqualified tribute to her abilities. The fact that Gertrude stayed with us throughout our Mallord Street days and only left when she found she couldn't bear life in the country; the fact that we had only two cooks in London – Mrs. Penn and Mrs. Gulliver; only two cooks at Cotchford – Mrs. Tasker (until a growing family compelled her to become a full-time mother) and Mrs. Wilson; only two gardeners (the first one blotting his copybook almost at once and having to be dismissed); only one Nanny: all bear testimony to this. And my mother was not only good with people. She was good with things, too. She had an eye for what was beautiful. It was her own eye, a natural eye, an untaught eye. She liked what she liked because she liked it, not because it was supposed to show good taste to like it. She didn't like antique furniture because she didn't like brown polished wood, and she particularly disliked mahogany. Brown was a dreary colour: she preferred gay colours – reds and yellows and greens. So she preferred painted furniture, and it didn't particularly matter whether it was old or new. It was nice to think that the chair she sat in to write her letters had come out of an ancient Venetian gondola, but it was equally nice to think that the wardrobe in her bedroom had been painted for her by a friend. The result of her labours was undoubtedly very lovely: at its best in the drawing-room and in her bedroom, but later on, when Peter Jones took it in hand, almost as good in the dining-room. At Peter Jones in the 1930s they were buying up ugly, heavy, Victorian, mahogany furniture – the sort of thing my mother most disliked – stripping off the polish and painting it in a style reminiscent of that of the Adam brothers. It was a treatment that fitted in very pleasingly with the pieces of old Italian painted furniture that a friend of my mother's (who ran a small antique shop) was occasionally able to acquire for her.

As a child I specially loved her bedroom. I loved to sit on the soft carpet in front of the gas fire drying myself after a bath. It was on top of her wardrobe that the Christmas parcels were put; and day by day I would watch the pile grow until at last, about a week before Christmas, I was allowed to start opening. One a day. Which one shall it be this morning? This one, large and square and rattly. My mother lifted it down and put it on the floor for me. Oh, unforgettable bliss, never to be recaptured!

At the top of the house was my nursery. We have already seen it through my childish eyes. An adult, visiting it, would find it no less pleasant: large, light, airy and gay, pleasingly furnished in a simple, modern style, a room designed – as a nursery should be – for doing things in, messy things, racketty things, rough-and-tumble things. . . .

At the back of the house on the same floor were two smaller rooms, side by side. One was shared by Gertrude and Mrs. Gulliver, the other was my father's bedroom. It was a very dark room and consequently only a very dim impression of it survives: an impression of ugly, heavy, Victorian, mahogany furniture, and of very little floor space in between. There were two pictures on the wall, or it may have been a double picture in a single frame. You could see them when you turned on the light. In the one a jaunty little man was taking his stance at the wicket: "The Hope of the Side". In the other was the same little man, but jaunty no longer: "Out First Ball". This was possibly the only thing in the whole room that really belonged to my father, the rest having been put there (so it seemed) because they had to go somewhere. As a boy these twin pictures used to make me smile. Today I still smile at the memory of them, but sadly now. Poor little cricketer! Do you remind me of somebody?

As a child one accepts without question that this room is the drawing-room, this the dining-room, that this is your bedroom and this mine. It never occurs that these are things that have to be decided. And certainly I would never have wondered who did the deciding, whether any one else was consulted and whether or not all were in favour.

Of course it was my mother who decided and my father who accepted – and who then made the discovery that once again the dampest, darkest, coldest, dingiest rooms had been reserved for him. I doubt if he ever complained, but I just don't know how much he silently minded.

One doesn't want to offer sympathy unnecessarily. If you are a writer what you want above all else is quiet. You don't in the least need gay, light, airy surroundings. A lot of sympathy is wasted on those who write in garrets. I am writing this in a garret, a small room that is utterly unlovely, that has never been decorated, never even *cleaned* since we came here twenty-two years ago. The plywood ceiling boards are sagging, the distemper is flaking off them and they are blotched with damp stains. The room is lit by a small skylight which also lets in the rain. There is no other lighting, there is no heating, and it is November. Yet I have chosen this room from all the others and it suits me perfectly. So I doubt if my father was sad about the rooms where he worked. I doubt if he ever wondered to himself when it might be their turn for a visit from the Peter

Jones man. Indeed, any complaining was more likely to come from my mother. "It really is just like a third class railway carriage in here." But his bedroom, surely, was different – his bedroom, dark, cramped and dismal, furnished, so it seemed, with what was left over, what wouldn't go anywhere else. . . .

Then there was his armchair by the fire in the drawing-room at Cotchford. All the other chairs were re-upholstered from time to time as they grew shabby, but somehow this chair always got overlooked. Sitting in it he had a slightly restless habit with his right elbow and over the years this had worn a hole not just through the cover but deep into the flock padding. Nothing was ever done about it. Now and then gentle hints were dropped: my father would never have gone further than that. But my mother's rather brusque reply was always the same: "Well, I don't really see that there's much point. You would only go and fidget another hole."

So perhaps somewhere here – in his armchair, in his little, north-facing bedroom at Cotchford, in his dark, cramped, dismal bedroom next door to Gertrude and Mrs. Gulliver in London – is to be found the original of Eeyore's Gloomy Place.

Most of us have small, sad places somewhere in our hearts and my father was no exception. Sometimes we let our feelings escape in bursts of anger. Sometimes we make long, dismal faces. My father did neither. He felt deeply but he kept his feelings to himself. Or rather, being a writer, he let them escape in his writing. But even here he disguised them, unable even in fiction to allow himself to take himself too seriously. And so such sadnesses as there were put on cap and bells and emerged as Eeyore, the old grey donkey. Eeyore is gloomy, but you can't feel sorry for him. You never long to make him happy. You know that it would be impossible, and that in any case he really prefers it that way. Silly old Eeyore to feel so sad in a world that is really so sunny and gay!

This book, as I said earlier, is a photograph album, a collection of snapshots. There is no place in it for an anatomical drawing. If the sad side of my father's life was kept from me as a child, I shall not now try to unearth it. Enough for me to be grateful that I knew only his smiles. Enough for others that he gave them Eeyore.

CHAPTER 20
Collaboration

"In August of that year (1920) my collaborator produced a more personal work."[1]

In those early days my father liked to think of himself and my mother as collaborators. His book, *Once a Week*, appearing in 1914, was dedicated to "my collaborator who buys the ink and paper, laughs, and in fact does all the really difficult part of the business." But of course this was not the collaboration that had produced the light verse that he and Ken had written together. My mother and father were not really collaborators at all in that sense: not in what my father wrote. Nor indeed in anything he did. Or rather only in one thing, and that was the work they jointly produced in 1920.

About sixteen years after that event I was standing with my father in front of the summerhouse at Cotchford when, thinking his thoughts aloud, he said: "You know, I often tell myself that everything we are is that way because that was how our parents made us. Every talent we have has been inherited. And this is something worth remembering if ever we feel ourselves getting

[1] *It's Too Late Now.*

a bit swanky. The credit is not ours: it is theirs. Not even theirs, really, but their parents'. And so on, back and back. And even if you say 'I had this talent and he had it too, but he wasted his and I used mine. Surely that is to my credit,' the answer is no. For if we make use of a talent it is only because we have another talent, a talent for using talents, a talent for hard work, if you like; and this too was inherited. . . ."

Perhaps one of the things I have inherited from my father is his attitude to pride. One is entitled to feel proud of something one has done if one genuinely believes one has done it well. One is entitled to feel inwardly proud of oneself for doing it well. One is even allowed to bask happily, though modestly, in the praise of others. But one is never entitled to be conceited, to be boastful, to display one's pride in public. It is conceit rather than pride that is the deadly sin. So that when we feel our pride bubbling up inside us, threatening to spill out into conceit, we must cork it down with the thought that, clever though we are, it is a cleverness that was given to us, not one of our own making. In this way we can perhaps look at ourselves dispassionately, with something of a Mendelian eye, seeing ourselves as the product of two people who have collaborated. Perhaps this thought may help us not just to suppress our pride but also to feel less unhappy about our failures; for if we have inherited all that is good in us we have also surely inherited all that is bad. If our talents came from our parents, so too did our un-talents; and this thought is con-soling.

Of course, inheritance is only where it starts; my father was well aware of this. Teaching played its part, and a very impor-tant part. A talent for cricket, a "natural eye", was not enough. Instinct won't tell you how to deal with an in-swinger on the leg stump. There must be coaching, long hours at the nets: "Head down, Milne. Nose over the ball." Teaching was vital if a talent was to be given its best chance. What brilliant son of a brilliant schoolmaster would not acknowledge that? Nor is it surprising that my father was, himself, a good teacher, and that I, like him, enjoyed learning.

First the talent, then the teaching. Lastly the luck. This, too, my father acknowledged, again and again. He had been lucky and he knew it. "My real achievement," he wrote, contemplating the fact that he had been made Assistant Editor of *Punch* at the age of 24, "was to be not wholly the wrong person in the right place at the right time." Luck! Like the dropped catch that enables you to go on to score fifty and so get a trial for the First Eleven. . . . Or equally the catch that wasn't dropped, and doomed you for ever to the Third Eleven.

If in this chapter I take the stage again, dressed now in grey flannel trousers and tweed jacket, and with my hair at last mercifully short, I do so as the product of that collaboration that started in 1920, and for the light which I hope it will throw on those two collaborators, my parents.

"And do you write, too?" he asked.

"No," I said.

"You haven't inherited any of your father's great gifts, then?"

"No," I said.

"Well, now. Isn't that extraordinary!"

No, I thought. But I kept quiet.

Why should it always be assumed that it is talents that are passed on and not un-talents? If my father had a talent for writing, my mother had an un-talent. Why should people always assume that I ought to have inherited the one rather than the other? If talents always dominated un-talents we should today be a world of Newtons, Shakespeares, Leonardos and saints. Blessed are the untalented!

Writing (so it seems to me) is a combination of two separate skills: the ability to use words and the ability to create with words; rather in the way that building a house demands two separate skills, the bricklayer's and the architect's. A writer, in other words, is simultaneously a craftsman and a designer.

If my father felt, as an undergraduate at Cambridge, an urge to be a writer, it was probably because he felt first an urge to create; and it was probably fortunate for him (and us) that this was an urge he could satisfy in no other way. Another man might have made things with his hands; my father made things with his imagination. If you haven't the creative urge or if it is satisfied elsehow, then, although you may be a skilled craftsman, writing the most delightful letters to your friends, the must lucid reports to your superiors, you will never produce a poem or a play or a story. You may make a journalist but you will never make an author.

Armed with this thought, let us now look dispassionately at the object which Mrs. Penn described so memorably on that August morning long ago as "tall like mistress". It is lying in its cradle, wrinkled and ugly. Suddenly, unseen by anyone, a Fairy appears, stoops over the cradle, waves her magic wand and casts her magic spell. "He shall have his father's brains and his mother's hands!" She speaks, then vanishes. The years pass by. The infant grows up. The spell begins to come true. Yes, she was a real Fairy all right. The only doubt is: was she the Good Fairy or was she the Bad Fairy? At first it seemed a blessing to be good at algebra and equally good at carpentry. "Versatile" was our word for it. Later, we talked about "strings to the bow". In the end I think we all had to admit to ourselves, if not to each other, that what a bow needs is one really good string, not two fairly good ones.

But as I have already said, my father never wanted me to be a writer. An artist, perhaps. An architect, perhaps. But not a writer. This great talent was all his own and not to be shared. Anyway, a ten-year-old schoolboy doesn't need to be thinking about his career just yet. Other things come first. Cricket, for instance.

Cricket, like football, is a game you can either play or (equally happily) watch. My father did both. He did most of his watching at the Oval, and as soon as I was old enough I accompanied him. I was about ten or eleven, and, if I remember, Woolley was batting at the time. . . . We lived in Chelsea and so should by rights have backed Middlesex, but my father's allegiance as a Londoner was always to Surrey. When we bought Cotchford he transferred most of it to Sussex; and I was for Sussex, too, wholeheartedly. Yet I never saw Sussex play. We never went to Hove. We never even watched a match at Tunbridge Wells, though it was only eight miles away and we went there often to shop. Our cricket watching was confined to the first two days of the summer holidays while we were still in London. Once we had moved down to Cotchford, though we would listen to the Test Match on the wireless – my father in the garden suddenly remembering, looking at his watch, giving a shout, galloping indoors, me following, enthusiastic, but with my enthusiasm never quite matching his – and though we would excitedly follow the fortunes of Sussex in the papers, we would never watch another first-class match. Why was this? Partly, I think, it was because he didn't want to have more than his fair share of me. If I was with him, then I was not with my mother. I played golf with him in the morning, I putted with him, played catch with him, and then in the evening we bowled at each other in the meadow. This was already almost more than his ration; and so, much as he might have liked to take me up to London to watch Surrey playing Sussex, it would have been wrong to do so. This was one reason, but there was, I think, another. Our visit to the Oval was more than just an opportunity to watch a game of cricket, just as the Green Sweet at the end of a meal was more than just the taste of peppermint. It was a ritual.

When, I wonder, did it all start? When did their father first take young Ken and Alan to the Oval, and who were the great ones they watched and whose fortunes they followed? Did they, too, confine their visits to the first days of the summer holidays? Did Ken and Alan continue these visits when they were grown up? Did Alan try taking Dorothy, hoping to make her an enthusiast too? Vain hope! So in the end Alan would have gone alone, taking only his memories, until at last the day came when I was old enough to join him, and the ritual could be re-established.

The turnstiles clicked as we went in. "Soft seats, sixpence! Soft seats, sixpence!" My father dug a shilling out of his pocket. "Match card! Card of the match! Match card!" From up here where we were sitting the distant voice had its own peculiar and memorable resonance. My father gesticulated to attract attention and gave his attention-catching whistle, and the voice came nearer. ... There's more to watching cricket than wondering who's going to win. Even the sparrows and the pigeons seem different here. Even the distant gasometers are lovely. Even the sky, palest blue patches showing between high, yellow-tinged clouds, is unique and unforgettable. And then, of course, there is the luncheon interval, and the battered leather attaché case can be put on the seat between us and opened. No need to wonder what is inside it: ham sandwiches, egg sandwiches and a paper bag full of cherries. This was how it always was. This, I suspect, was how it had always been. And while I looked forward happily to eight whole weeks of Cotchford, my father, equally happily, looked back. ...

Two days at the Oval and then down to Cotchford to try out some of the strokes I had been watching; to be C. F. Walters flicking his wrists and sending the ball past extra cover to the boundary; to be Frank Woolley sweeping a long hop over mid-wicket's head. If I never became a good cricketer (and I never became a good cricketer) no one could say it was for lack of instruction. In fact I suppose one might fairly say it was from over-instruction. My road to the Third Eleven began during the Christmas holidays when I was nine years old. The South African cricketer, Major J. A. Faulkner, was running a cricket school somewhere in South London, and thither Burnside drove us, my father and me, four mornings a week.

Here I was put in the charge of T. B. Reddick and shown how
to make the forward defensive stroke. By the end of the holidays
I could play forward defensively and I could also follow through
with a flick of the wrists when the good length ball was a half
volley. The following May, armed with these two strokes, I
went to my new prep school, and to my slight disappointment
found them of only limited value. However, next Christmas
I learned the back stroke. Subsequently, when Faulkners
closed down, we moved to a school run by Sandham and
Strudwick, and I progressed to square cuts, late cuts, hooks
and glides. And I may say that I cut and hooked, glided and
drove with considerable skill and elegance. So that if this was
all there was to cricket I felt fairly confident that one day I
would be playing for England.

Unfortunately, however, there are other things: things like
not getting out first ball and like making runs; even totally
different things like fielding and not dropping catches. And
here my skill deserted me. Cricket, one might say, makes two
requirements of its practitioners: a co-ordination of hand and
eye and the right temperament. I had the one but not the other.
It was not just that I was content to be graceful and elegant
without bothering about runs (though this was partly the
trouble). It was that I trembled. And, as the cricket master at
Boxgrove once pointed out to me: "The Captain of the First
Eleven, taking his stance at the wicket, just ought not to
tremble." I also trembled when a catch came my way, so that
I nearly always dropped it. Once I had got past the trembling
stage, had scored half a dozen runs and got my eye in, I might
well end up with a creditable innings. And if, in the field,
a ball was hit at me so hard that I hadn't time to start worrying
I might very well bring off a brilliant one-handed catch.
Nervousness! That was what kept me in the Third Eleven at
Stowe. Bad luck as well, of course, like that time I played
slightly across my second ball trying to hit it past mid-on. . . .

But mainly, I must now admit, just nervousness. Inherited, naturally, which is a consolation. . . .

Grandfather Milne was nervous. Not nervous or shy or awkward with boys; only with grown-ups. "His shyness became apparent to us," wrote my father,[1] "when we went out walking together and met an acquaintance. As soon as the acquaintance was sighted Papa would cut short his conversation, or ours, and prepare for the ordeal. The funny story, the explanation of the Force of Gravity, our answer to a catch-question had to wait. . . . He let my hand go, and put his own up to his hat. 'Good morning, Mr. Roberts, good morning to you, good morning.' Mr. Roberts returned the greeting and passed, but Papa's greeting went on. His hand still went up and down to his hat in nervous movements, he still muttered 'Good morning to you.'"

Some of his shyness was passed on to my father, but not enough to make him awkward or embarrassed or unhappy; enough only to prevent him from being a ready mixer, the life and soul of the party; enough to keep him behind his *Times* on a train journey; and enough, fortunately, to make him sympathize with me. For if the Milne shyness retreated when it reached my father, it did so the better to attack when my turn came.

And what an opportunity it found! An only child, oddly dressed, odd hair style, odd name, the hero of a nursery story. "Hullo, Christopher Robin! Still saying your prayers?"

An only child needs someone to cling to. I began by clinging to my Nanny. I clung so tightly that she became almost a part of me, so that when I was told one August afternoon that I was to spend a fortnight with Anne and her family on the Kent coast and that Nanny would not be coming with me, I lay down on the ground and howled: and the memory of that howling is still vivid.

[1] *It's Too Late Now.*

But tiny children are often shy. This is quite natural and nothing to worry about. They grow out of it eventually. With such thoughts my parents no doubt reassured themselves.

When I was nine Nanny left. I was still as shy as ever; worse, if anything. I still needed someone to cling to. So I clung to my father. For nearly ten years I had clung to Nanny. For nearly ten more years I was to cling to him, adoring him as I had adored Nanny, so that he too became almost a part of me, at first, no doubt, to his delight, later perhaps to his anxiety. "Do I, Nanny?" I had asked when I was a child and Nanny had provided the answer. Now my father was providing the answer, not because I didn't know it, but because I couldn't say it. Around the age of eight – and not altogether surprisingly – my voice had begun to get itself knotted up. By the age of twelve, though I was fluent on occasions, there were other occasions when the words got themselves sadly jammed. By the age of sixteen the jamming had got worse, and my shyness wasn't helping things. Grandfather Milne could at least say "Good morning"; I would have stuck at the "G", and, aware of an insurmountable "G" approaching me down the road, I would have hurried up a side street to avoid it. What does a parent do in such circumstances? Does he (for example) say "If you want it you must go and buy it yourself."? Or does he say "All right, let's go and buy it together."? Rightly or wrongly, it was the latter that my father did, and I blessed him for it and loved him all the more.

So there I was, very close indeed to my father, adoring him, admiring him, accepting his ideas, yet at the same time immensely sensitive, easily wounded, quick to take offence. An accidental word of reproof or criticism from him and tears would stream from my eyes and a barrier of silence would descend between us keeping us apart for days. So he had to be careful what he said. But provided he was careful I was, I imagine, an easy child to teach. His knowledge, his opinions, his beliefs could be passed on to me and I would eagerly accept them as my own. It was too easy, almost. In fact it was dangerously easy.

My father used to say that the third-rate brain thought with the majority, the second-rate brain thought with the minority and the first-rate brain thought for itself. His was, and he wanted mine to be, a first-rate brain. There were facts that he could teach me: facts that were not in dispute, like how to bowl a leg break or solve a quadratic equation. But where there was uncertainty, where opinions differed, here I would have to think and decide for myself. And perhaps the largest, most fundamental and most vital area of uncertainty lay in what one believed about God.

If you had talked to my father about his religious beliefs (and if he had been prepared to discuss them with you) you might have concluded that he was a Humanist. But of course he would have objected to the label as he would object to any label that seemed to put him among a class of people all thinking alike. He might have preferred to be described as an agnostic, since this was a purely negative definition, describing what he was not. As to what he was, as to what exactly he did believe, this, in the end, he recorded in his book *The Norman Church*. But *The Norman Church* was not written until 1948 when he was approaching seventy. Up to this his views had been his own affair, kept almost entirely to himself.

As to my views, I have already boldly stated what I thought they were at the age of three; and they remained substantially the same for the next fifteen years. In other words, here was I a Believer, and here was my father an Unbeliever, and somewhere in between (and I never discovered exactly where) was my mother. An awkward situation? Not particularly. My father was quite happy that my religious education should be the conventional one (and my mother was no doubt only too happy to leave such difficult matters to him to decide). If my Nanny wanted to teach me to say my prayers, she could. If at school one did Divinity and went to Chapel, then it was far better that I should join the others than be the odd one out. For I was quite odd enough already. So provided he did not have to compromise his own beliefs and provided no irrevocable decisions were taken that might affect mine, he was prepared to let things take their course. This meant that, though I was given two Christian names, I was never christened. Nor (naturally) was I confirmed. I was too young to be aware of this first omission, but the second one puzzled me at the time, not really knowing the reason. Puzzled me and left me a little unhappy, but nothing more than that.

When is a young person old enough to make up his mind for himself? When is his mind sufficiently developed to be able to weigh up all the arguments and not merely fall for the one that is most persuasively put? Certainly not when he is only sixteen.

My father waited until I was twenty-four. The war was on. I was in Italy. From time to time he used to send me parcels of books to read. In one of them were two in the Thinker's Library series: Renan's *The Life of Jesus* and Winwood Reade's *The Martyrdom of Man*. I started with *The Life of Jesus* and found it quite interesting; I turned to *The Martyrdom* and found it enthralling. From the very first paragraph I felt myself seized and swept along on Winwood Reade's tumultuous prose, through War, through Religion, through Liberty, to Intellect, finding at every stage the answers to all my questions, the resolutions of all the doubts that, over the past five years, had begun to gather. Then, after so much had been explained, after so much had been destroyed, came the new picture. In Reade's words: ". . . the colours blend and harmonize together and we see that the picture represents One Man." One Man! Mankind! There was no God. God had not created Man in His own image. It was the other way round: Man had created God. And Man was all there was. But it was enough. It was the answer, and it was both totally convincing and totally satisfying. It convinced and satisfied me as I lay in my tent somewhere on the narrow strip of sand that divides Lake Comacchio from the Adriatic; and it has convinced and satisfied me ever since.

I wrote at once to my father to tell him so and he at once wrote back. And it was then that I learned for the first time that these were his beliefs, too, and that he had always hoped that one day I would come to share them. But he had not wanted to put any pressure on me. For twenty-four years he had been willing to allow the Church a free hand to use all its influence and persuasiveness (though never its force, and that was why I had not been christened), while he himself had remained silent. But now, he had felt, the time had come for me to decide, for me to hear the other side and then to make up my mind. So he had sent me *The Martyrdom*. But even then he had wanted to play absolutely fair, and so he had added *The Life of Jesus*. And then he had been content to leave the verdict to me. Well, he said, the Church had done its best. It had had twenty-four years start – and it had failed.

I read the letter many times. It joined the others in my battledress pocket and was in its turn joined by yet others until the pocket bulged too much. . . .

If I had to compile a list of "Books that have Influenced my Life", high on the list would undoubtedly be Winwood Reade's *Martyrdom of Man*. And it would probably be equally high on my father's list too. If you read a book and it influences you greatly, or even if you just enjoy it very much, you long to persuade others to read it too. A book is not just to be read privately in the evening in front of the fire. It is a pleasure to be shared, it is the cement that bonds person to person in greater sympathy and understanding. It was, after all, their shared love of the light verse of C. S. Calverley and Owen Seaman that helped to bring my parents together. (Admittedly Seaman was both my father's Editor and my mother's God-father, but their delight was genuine, and for years after he had relinquished these responsibilities they continued to quote from and laugh at his verses).

You can learn a lot about people by running your eye over the books they keep in their bookshelves. There were books by the thousand at Mallord Street and Cotchford: gardening books that my mother loved, detective stories that were my father's passion, the complete works of this or that famous writer, Lord Edward Gleichen's *London's Open Air Statuary* (a puzzling one unless you knew the reason[1]), and many, many more. Impossible to look at them all, so let us just glance at a small handful.

When I first made my appearance Calverley and Seaman were of course beyond me and would have to wait. But I could make an early start with Edward Lear and Lewis Carroll. Of the two my mother preferred Lear, my father Carroll. Carroll's verses are technically the better and this partly accounts for my father's taste. But they are also happier, more light-hearted, and this was, I think, another reason. Lear, though funny, is at the same time deeply tragic. You can laugh but you can also cry at the Yonghy Bonghy Bò, the Jumblies, the Dong and the Pobble, even at Calico Pie. My mother cried very readily, an easy prey to her emotions. She was emotional but not shy. My father on the other hand was shy but not noticeably emotional. I, inheriting from each, was both. This difference between my parents can be seen again in a book that we all greatly loved and admired and read aloud or alone, over and over and over: *The Wind in the Willows*. This book is, in a way, two separate books spliced into one. There are, on the one hand, those chapters concerned with the adventures of Toad; and on the other hand there are those chapters that explore human emotions – the emotions of fear, nostalgia, awe,

[1] Fellow soldiers during the War (he was my father's Divisional Commander), and near neighbours afterwards, they had exchanged works. Equally surprising must have seemed the presence of *Winnie the Pooh* among the General's books.

wanderlust. My mother was drawn to the second group, of which 'The Piper at the Gates of Dawn' was her favourite, read to me again and again with always, towards the end, the catch in the voice and the long pause to find her handkerchief and blow her nose. My father, on his side, was so captivated by the first group that he turned these chapters into the children's play, *Toad of Toad Hall*. In this play one emotion only is allowed to creep in: nostalgia. And for as long as I knew him this was the only emotion that he seemed to delight in both feeling and showing.

So it is not surprising that it was he who pressed *Treasure Island* into my hands, while my mother read me *At the Back of the North Wind*. And Wodehouse was something at which we could all three laugh happily together in the drawing-room after dinner.

A schoolboy needs guidance on what to read. I remember, after my first glance at the library at Stowe, writing home to say it seemed to consist almost entirely of the Works of Burke in about 500 volumes. My father was only too glad to recommend something a little lighter and I was only too glad to take his advice. I worked my way through Wells, through Dickens and through Hardy, each leaving a very deep and enduring impression on me as, presumably, they had on him. If one were to say what these three writers shared in common it might possibly be that all three wrote about dustmen rather than dukes and wrote about them with understanding and compassion. The de Selincourts (dare I make this sweeping generalization?) liked to think of themselves as aristocrats who had fled from the Revolution. The Milnes were proud of the fact that Grandfather was poor and Great Grandfather even poorer. In this I was a Milne, not a de Selincourt, and I and my father felt the keenest sympathy for Kipps, for young Copperfield, for Oak when he was penniless, for Henchard when he was ruined.

So, one by one, with my father as guide, I scaled the heights of English Literature. Only Poetry, that range that thrusts up some of the greatest heights of all, did we skirt around. I wonder why? Shall I make a guess?

When my father had reached an age when he could reasonably feel that it was not unbecoming to take himself seriously in public (he was then 70) he had this to say of serious poetry:[1]

> I saw old Autumn in the misty morn
> Stand shadowless like Silence, listening
> To Silence

Kipling (or a character in one of his stories) said that there were just five transcendent lines of enchantment in poetry; lines giving what Quiller-Couch called the Great Thrill. Two of these are known to everybody:

> Charmed magic casements opening on the foam
> Of perilous seas in faery lands forlorn.

The other three, not perhaps quite so well known, are:

> A savage place, as holy and enchanted
> As ever 'neath a waning moon was haunted
> By woman wailing for her demon lover.

On my own account (continued my father) I add to them the lines with which I began, together with those earlier ones from "Kubla Khan":

> Where Alph the sacred river ran
> Through caverns measureless to man
> Down to a sunless sea

and

> While Ilion like a mist rose into towers.

If these five passages have anything in common, what is it? I think it is that they transport us immediately into an

[1] *Year in, Year Out.*

experience which we seem to have known, in fact or imagination, all our lives.

In other words, poetry for my father opened casements not on to new but on to old landscapes, reawakening old, dim, half-forgotten memories. In a single word, poetry was nostalgic.

Perhaps because one man's nostalgia is not another's, because the memories poetry stirred in him could never be the memories it stirred in me, and because his memories were his most private possession – perhaps it was for these reasons that serious poetry remained in our family no more than something that my father was good at when it came to solving the quotations in *The Times* crossword.

So, leaving poetry behind us, we come to the last book in my list. It was a list that began with a book that influenced my life very greatly in one sort of way. It ends with a book that influenced it equally greatly in a different sort of way. A book can be either a signpost pointing in a new (and hopefully better) direction, or it can be a companion keeping one company, year in, year out, through all life's twisting ways. The first sort of book one reads once, the second over and over again. For me *The Martyrdom* was the first sort, *Bevis* the second.

Bevis, The Story of a Boy, by Richard Jefferies, though still in print, is not, alas, a book that many boys now read. So perhaps Bevis fans will forgive me if I explain to the others that Jefferies was a naturalist and that the book describes in fictional form his boyhood on a Wiltshire farm. Bevis and his companion, Mark, play at savages, soldiers and explorers, explore rivers, woods and islands, build a raft and a hut, make a matchlock gun, learn to swim and to sail, squabble and make it up, brood, dream, stare up at the night sky and down to the meadow flowers growing at their feet. In short they do all the things that I was either doing or wanting to do.

Though this was a book that my father put into my hands (literally: I remember his doing it), he did so saying it was a present from my grandfather; that it was my grandfather who specially wanted me to read it and who hoped I was now old enough to get from it the pleasure it had given him. And having done this, he did no more; and *Bevis* became and remained always a personal and private pleasure that I have made almost no attempt to share with anyone else. The book was published in 1882, the year my father was born. So my grandfather must have first read it when he was already a father and must have then urged it on his sons. Did any of the three share his enthusiasm? Certainly my father didn't, nor really is this surprising. For though Bevis had Mark for his constant companion, and though Jefferies had a younger brother, this is really the autobiography of a solitary, lonely boy and so makes its appeal to other solitaries. I have known only two other Bevis fans. I can see what they and I had in common, and I can guess what it is that gives this book its particular appeal to the likes of us. It is the author's relationship with the countryside, with nature. If there are two of you and you are really together, as Ken and Alan were together, then the country is your playground where you exercise your muscle. You plan walks and bicycle rides, and afterwards you boast about the distances you have covered. You scramble up rocks in order to be able to report that you got to the top. But if you are alone, then the country is not your playground, it is your companion; and nature becomes Nature, a person, someone to whom you can almost talk. You do not only walk through measured miles; you sit, dreaming, contemplating, absorbing it all, through unmeasured minutes. Your eye does not only identify the snipe flying overhead or spot the whitethroat's nest, it notices and remembers the pink tips on the petals of the daisy.

I was shy, solitary, awkward in company, inarticulate in speech, becoming worse as I grew older. How lucky, then, I was to have parents who understood, who felt that, though perhaps what I needed for my own ultimate good was to be thrown in at the deep end, this was where, happily or otherwise, I was spending my term-time, so that during the holidays it was only kind to allow me to enjoy myself in the shallows. How lucky I was to have Cotchford for four blissful weeks at Easter and eight even more blissful weeks in the summer, and to have it almost entirely to myself. If someone came to tea – and sometimes someone came to tea – I need do no more that put in an appearance, then slide silently off, down to the river, to look for crossing places. . . .

Alone by the river, alone through the fields, alone in Posingford, alone in the depths of the Five Hundred Acre, alone on the top of the Forest. Sitting alone on the grass in the sunshine. Walking alone through the woods at night. Alone with myself. Alone – yet never lonely. What bliss this was!

CHAPTER 21
The Pistol

I ended the last chapter by referring to *Bevis*. Reading *Bevis* is a little like spending the evening at the local cinema. It doesn't enormously matter where you come in, you simply see the film round to that point. If you wish, you can then see it on again to the end. And if you are really keen, or your seat is particularly comfortable, you can start once more at the beginning. . . .

I have always found it difficult to stop reading *Bevis*. It is a circular book, the last chapter being the chapter before the first; and it needs a real effort to say "Enough" and to put it back on the shelf. As a boy, of course, I simply stopped when the holidays came to an end, then started again the following holidays. The book remained permanently on my bedside table at Cotchford, read daily every morning while waiting for my father to appear and announce that the bathroom was empty.

I mention this to explain why, although I thought I had dealt adequately with the book in the last chapter, it seems determined to make an appearance in this chapter as well.

This time, however, it is not Bevis, the boy, I am concerned with, but his father, "the Governor". Bevis, Jefferies and the reader are all, I think, deeply conscious of the vitally important part played by the Governor, even though, as a character, he scarcely appears. For a boy like Bevis he was all that a father should be: deeply caring for his son, anxious to encourage in him the growth of self-reliance and initiative, knowing that a boy learns better what he teaches himself, willing to let him take risks, believing that a father should be felt rather than seen, should watch but seldom interfere.

He interferes only twice: first to teach the boys to swim and later (having first watched their vain struggles) to give them a small piece of advice on sailing.

In many ways I was different from Bevis, and my father was even more different from the Governor. But the two men had this in common: they trusted their sons.

Once when a friend of my parents' was lunching with us, she asked what I did with myself all day. My father answered for me that I spent a lot of my time just wandering about.

"You let him go where he likes?"

"Yes."

"You're not afraid he might get into danger?"

"No. He knows how to look after himself."

There are a hundred ways in which a boy can injure – if not indeed kill – himself. The more adventurous he is and the greater his initiative, the more ways he will find. If you protect him from each of the hundred, he is sure to find the hundred and first. Though most men can look back on their boyhood and tremble at the narrowness of some of their escapes, most boys do in fact survive more or less intact, and the wise father is the trusting father. My father's trust was so natural that I never thought about it or about the anxiety that must often have lain behind it. Take the following story, for instance: the story of my pistol.

One day Robin and I (Robin was a friend of mine: we were both about nine years old at the time) were playing in the gardens outside the Natural History Museum in London when we became aware of another boy who was engaged in firing a pistol. It was the sound that attracted our attention. For it was not the feeble popping of a cap pistol, but an ear-splitting explosion – quite the real thing. We went over to him to get a closer look. He fired again: it was most impressive. We asked him if we could see it, and proudly he showed it to us. We asked where he had bought it, and he told us.

Robin had the sort of parents who don't usually say no. So it was agreed that he should put the matter to them. And shortly afterwards the two pistols were produced and two boxes of blank cartridges, one for each of us. To try them out I was invited to Richmond Park; and while Robin's mother sat on the grass surrounded by the remains of our picnic, he and I battled with his father over a fallen tree trunk. Afterwards his father said: "If those had been real pistols I'd have been riddled with bullets through and through." Riddled with bullets: what wonderful, memorable words.

A year or two later, at Cotchford, I was looking at my pistol, still as beloved as ever. It was small and simple, but well and solidly and safely made. You could fire it point blank at an enemy without too much risk because it discharged downwards through a hole in the underside of the barrel near its tip. The tip itself was blocked. So you couldn't in fact load it with anything other than blank cartidges, which was a pity – unless, of course, you filed the tip off. I had a file, and set to work.

The file cut through the metal quite easily and soon the job was done and the end smoothed off. Then I loaded with a blank cartridge and pushed three or four gimp pins down the barrel. The cupboard where I kept my tools would do for a target. I stood a yard or two away and pulled the trigger. The noise indoors was deafening. I looked at the cupboard and was pleased to see that it was nicely riddled with gimp pins. This was a satisfactory start. The next step was to see about getting some better cartridges, cartridges with bullets.

My contact for this sort of thing was Mitchell's Garage. The two brothers who ran it – one fat, one thin – were useful allies. For without some sort of help I was a bit stuck: both Tunbridge Wells and East Grinstead being beyond my range. So a message was passed to Mitchell's – probably via Mrs. Wilson – and eventually (oh, wonderful day!) a message came back that the cartridges awaited my collection. I put my pistol in my pocket, called for Pat (Mrs. Wilson's daughter) and together we set off up the lane.

Mitchell's Garage was a large, barn-like structure with room for lots of cars inside it, but on this occasion it was more or less empty. The cartridges looked fine, with round, lead bullets sticking out of their ends. I stood in the middle of the garage and loaded. I had a bit of difficulty getting the cartridge to go right in: it went most of the way, then jammed. But by slightly loosening a screw I was able to get the breech mechanism to close behind it. Then I pulled the trigger. There was a loud explosion, an alarming flash and a violent stinging sensation in my hand. I dropped the pistol with a cry and found the back of my hand spattered with gunpowder and blood. Luckily the damage was not serious and I turned my attention to the pistol. What had gone wrong? At once I saw. The hole in the barrel was not big enough. That was why I had been unable to push the cartridge in properly in the first place. I ought to have seen this at the time. The bullet had stuck and the explosion backfired. Tragedy! I took the pistol to Mr. Mitchell. What could he do? Was it possible to drill out the barrel? He looked at it, said he though it was, and together we went into his workshop. With the barrel drilled out, the cartridges fitted perfectly and I was all set to try another shot then and there, but rather to my surprise Mr. Mitchell said "No, no. Please! Not here!" and hurried me outside. So I kept my first shot for a gate on the way home that had a notice on it saying "Private".

The pistol now worked beautifully and I could fire it at all sorts of things, though only at inanimate things. Neither my father nor I ever took any pleasure in killing, and hated those who did. So mostly I aimed at trees and sometimes I let Pat aim too, and once I even allowed my father to aim. I aimed and usually I missed. The pistol wasn't as accurate as I had hoped. Perhaps it needed sights. So I made a foresight and a backsight with bits of wire twisted round the barrel and then glued. Then I found an old plywood target and took it down to the river and hung it from a branch of the oak tree. I fired, expecting the target to be knocked sideways by the impact, but nothing happened. Had I missed? I went closer and fired again. Again nothing. This was very disappointing. My sights must be wrong. I went still closer . . . and then I saw the two neat holes going clean through the plywood, and I was thrilled.

So that was my pistol and for a year or two it gave me immense pleasure. Then one day at breakfast my father said: "Do you remember John Wetherell? I've just heard from his father that he's lost an eye. He was playing with a gun and it went off in his face." An awful, icy feeling hit me in the stomach. John was a boy I used to play cricket with, a wonderful batsman, one of my heroes. "He *could* go on playing cricket, of course. You *can* play cricket with only one eye. Ranji did, as you know. But his father has thrown in his hand, doesn't want him ever to play again." A pause while this awful story sank in and spread its message throughout my entire body, down into my feet and into the tips of my fingers. Then, very gently my father added: "That's why I've never been too happy about your pistol."

Nothing more was said or needed to be said. After breakfast I put pistol, box of cartridges and a screwdriver into my pocket and went down to the river. I chose a place where the water was deepest. I threw the cartridges in first, one at a time, scattering them here and there over the surface of the water. Then with the screwdriver I took my pistol to bits. There were five pieces, and, walking down the river bank, I chose five separate places for them, so that they could never come together again, threw them in, watched them sink.

Then I came home.

CHAPTER 22
The Ointment Round the Fly

One of my father's favourite stories is about an old lady and a snake-charmer. The story is not his: he heard it from a friend. But I will leave him to tell it in his own words. The old lady and her husband were visiting a fair at which one of the attractions was an Indian snake-charmer's tent:

It so happened that at the moment when all the snakes had come out of their box to gather round the snake-charmer and sway to his pipings, he was overcome by illness, dropped his pipe, and fell back unconscious. The snakes, no longer under control, and looking elsewhere for amusement, started a panic among the spectators; but before the children could be thoroughly trampled underfoot, the old lady stepped forward, took up the pipe, sat cross-legged on the ground, and gave the snakes the music they loved. They hurried back to listen, rapt; and one by one she picked them up and returned them to their box.

As she and her husband were leaving the tent, followed by an enthusiastic and now intrepid crowd, he said to her:

"Why, Mary darling, we have known each other for

more than fifty years, and you never told me you could charm snakes!"

And the old lady said: "You never asked me, John."[1]

Perhaps what gave this story its particular appeal to my father was that he was a Mary-ish person himself, reluctant to volunteer personal information, preferring to wait and be asked, waiting often in vain. And the same is true of me.

We have both at times been utterly bored listening to others talking about themselves. We have both of us felt, on occasions, "What a show-off that man was". We have both of us been terrified of being thought either bores or show-offs. And so we have preferred silence.

My father wrote *It's Too Late Now* in 1938 when he was fifty-six. It is subtitled "The Autobiography of a Writer" but it isn't really that at all. It is the story of a boy. A third of the book covers only the first eleven years of his life: half the book the first eighteen years. "When I read the biography of a well-known man," he wrote in his introduction, "I find that it is the first half of it which holds my attention. . . . Tell us why the boy became an apothecary, and how the apothecary found himself writing 'Endymion', and let us guess for ourselves that the author of 'Endymion' will meet Wordsworth and Shelley, and surprise neither of them with an 'Ode to a Nightingale'. . . . Feeling like this about other people I feel like it also about myself."

He wrote his autobiography to please himself. He is not telling the reader how he became a great writer. He is not boasting of his successes. He does not give us a list of the famous people he rubbed shoulders with. The Pooh books occupy only eight rather unhappy pages. No, he wrote his autobiography because it gave him an opportunity to return to his boyhood – a boyhood from which all his inspiration sprang. It was in a sense his last visit: for I was now eighteen.

[1] *Year in, Year out.*

Let me explain.

When We Were Very Young and *Now We Are Six*: the titles trip from the tongue and we scarcely pause to ask ourselves who exactly is meant by "we". It is, of course, the obvious pronoun. "He" might have done instead but would have been a bit limiting. "They" is a bit condescending. "I" and "you" are clearly wrong. So only "we" remains. But that still leaves the question "Who is we?". Is it the "we" with which so many adults address the young? "And how are we today?" Heaven forbid! Is it then the universal "we": all of us – for whatever our age now we were all young once? Possibly this was how it was meant to seem. But I guess that in his heart my father intended it for just two people: himself and his son.

My father, who had derived such happiness from his childhood, found in me the companion with whom he could return there. But with Nanny in the way he could only take his dream son and return in imagination – to mend a train or keep a dormouse or go fishing. When I was three he was three. When I was six he was six. We grew up side by side and as we grew so the books were written. Then when I was nine and he was nine Nanny left. We could now do real things together: reality could in part replace the dream. For the next nine years we continued to grow up alongside each other. I was not aware of this, of course. I just saw him as my father. But he, I now suspect, saw me as a sort of twin brother, perhaps a sort of reincarnation of Ken. I – as I have already mentioned – needed him. He no less but for a different reason needed me. He needed me to escape from being fifty. It was a private dream of his, but he did once share it. I say once but I really mean in one place. The place was Dorset.

Up to now I have made no mention of Ken's family. Oddly, they didn't enter my life until I was fourteen – the year of the first Dorset visit. Ken's illness and death – when I was eight – may have been part of the reason, but mainly I suspect it was because his children – my cousins – were all so much older than

I was. What has an eight-year-old in common with a thirteen-year-old? But as I grew up the gap would have lessened. And so when I was fourteen there came a letter from Aunt Maud. It was August. We were at Cotchford; and they, so she told us, were renting a house by the sea at Osmington near Weymouth. "It has a flat roof where you can sunbathe and there is a swallow's nest under the porch. Won't you come and join us?" Shall we? Just the two of us? It might be rather fun. "Oh, do let's," I said. So we did. We bought maps. We studied them. We planned the route. We calculated distances. We prepared a "schedule" (a word which for this purpose my father pronounced "skeddle"). And then early one sunny morning we departed. He drove. I was the map reader. Our luggage was in the dicky behind us. We stopped for plums at Billingshurst. We turned left instead of right at Trickett's Cross – and I was in disgrace. We lunched at an inn at Midhurst – and there's no need for me to say what we ate. And in the early evening we arrived at Osmington and there were Maud, Angela, Tim, Tony and the swallow to welcome us.

This was the first of four such visits. My mother joined us briefly on the second but was not at her ease. Anne was happily with us on the last. Others came and went but mostly it was just the six of us: a boy just beginning at his public school, a young man at Oxford, another young man in his first job, a young woman wondering about marriage, a middle-aged mother and a middle-aged father. How did we all fit in together? What did we find to do all day? Well, we had the sea, of course, just a short walk away, offering rocks to clamber over and rock pools to hunt for creatures in. Further off was a beach to which we could take a picnic lunch, towels and bathing dresses. On two occasions we had a tennis court, and on one occasion a couple of dogs had been left behind by their owners to entertain us. But this still left plenty of time for wondering what to do next; and it still left the catering and cleaning to be organized. I came from a home where these things looked after themselves, or rather they were looked after by cooks and maids. But at Osmington there were no cooks or maids. So how did we manage? Like this.

Maud presided. She was mother to us all, a regal figure moving quietly in the background. She and the scrambled eggs were there at breakfast. She and the ham salad were there at supper. In between, while we were lying happily on the beach, idly throwing stones into the water, I imagine that she was busy fixing things with the grocer and the milkman. If floors needed to be swept I imagine that it was she who swept them; if dishes had to be washed, she who washed them. But I hope (because I cannot now recall) that if beds were to be made I at least made my own. Maud, aged about fifty, remained fifty. The rest of us became children.

Perhaps it was Tim's discovery of an Angela Brazil story in the bookshelf that started it. We joked about it. Some of us read it. And then, quite naturally, quite unself-consciously, we slipped back through the years to our schooldays. I would put our age at around twelve. Five twelve-year-olds playing happily together. I don't for a moment think that this was done deliberately in order to level out our assorted ages. Nor do I think that it was my father who led us back. I think it just happened because we were all Milnes and this is a thing that Milnes can do. We do it without effort and we do it for our own private delight. There is no winking at the audience; no "Look at me playing with the kiddies." For us, to whom our childhood has meant so much, the journey back is short, the coming and going easy.

Our Dorset became the world of Angela Brazil, of the Fifth Form at St. Dominics, of schoolboy slang and schoolboy ideals, where prep was a swot to be cut if poss, where you battled on the playing field for the honour of the House. And somewhere there still survives a photograph of us, the Owls, a small, earnest, idealistic Boy Scout/Girl Guide Troop posing in front of the camera . . . and not so very unlike those thousands of group photographs that line the walls of hundreds of prep schools today.

The Owls! We even had our special Owl Song. It was written when summer had faded, when our valiant deeds were but a memory, when I was back at Stowe and the others were gathered round the fireside one evening in London.

It was in collaboration with Ken that my father started writing light verse. How appropriate that this, the only other time he collaborated, should have been with Ken's children. Four lines only survive unforgotten, and so they had better be entitled:

THE OWLS – A Fragment

Look for the rainbow in the sky!
Look for the kidney in the pie!
Look for the ointment round the fly!
Rally, Owls! Rally!

On the whole it doesn't make a bad motto for us Milnes.

Epilogue

If the Pooh books had been like most other books – published one year, forgotten the next – there would have been no problem. If I had been a different sort of person there might well have been no problem. Unfortunately the fictional Christopher Robin refused to die and he and his real-life namesake were not always on the best of terms. For the first misfortune (as it sometimes seemed) my father was to blame. The second was my fault.

Actually it was not one but two problems. First: Christopher Robin and the Schoolboy; secondly: Christopher Robin and the Man. The two are separated not just in time but by the fact that two quite different sides of my personality were the cause.

Take the Schoolboy first. This was by far the lesser of the two. It was a problem caused by my shyness. I have already said that this was Grandfather Milne's responsibility rather than my father's: that I would have been plagued by shyness anyway, Christopher Robin or no. Nevertheless, Christopher Robin undoubtedly made things worse, though perhaps less so than might have been supposed. His appearances at school were few. Mostly we were occupied with other things, other anxieties, other delights. Fridays, for instance, were clouded by the thought of Latin, Latin, Maths, Soup, Fish, Biscuits, P.T., History, French. If I fussed over the Fish and dreaded the History this had nothing to do with a boy and his bear. Nevertheless, Christopher Robin was beginning to be what he was later to become, a sore place that looked as if it would never heal up. To begin with it was only sometimes sore; at other times it was quite the reverse. It would depend, of course, on the intentions of the person who raised the subject. If he intended to hurt, he could do so quite easily, for I was very vulnerable. I vividly recall how intensely painful it was to me to sit in my study at Stowe while my neighbours played the famous – and now cursed – gramophone record remorselessly over and over again. Eventually, the joke, if not the record, worn out, they handed it to me, and I took it and broke it into a hundred fragments and scattered them over a distant field. But mostly I had other things to think about and didn't bother about being Christopher Robin one way or the other. And because I spent so much time at school not bothering and the entire holidays not bothering, it never occurred to me that perhaps I ought to be blaming somebody for it all. In fact I blamed nobody. I felt no resentment. My relations with my father were quite unaffected.

Christopher Robin and the Man is a less happy story. Here the cause of the trouble was jealousy.

My father was lucky in that this was something that could have clouded, but in fact did not, his earlier relations with his brother, Ken. Alan, sixteen months his junior, was intellectually his superior. Ken was clever, Alan cleverer. Ken was successful, Alan even more successful. All through their very happy lives together Alan was always to beat Ken, yet Ken was never to feel resentment. How fortunate for the two of them that the talents had been dealt out in this way, that if one of them had to suffer from jealousy it was Alan (who didn't need to), not Ken. How nice if, when my turn came, I could have been another Ken. How sad that I wasn't.

As a schoolboy my jealousy was directed mainly against my contemporaries. I was jealous when Tompkins minor made more runs that I did and got into the Second Eleven while I remained in the Third. But luckily I was brainier than he and this consoled me. At home I was only jealous of my father when he beat me at golf. The rest of the time we were not rivals but friends. The sun shone equally upon us both. Neither stood in the other's shadow.

But in 1947 all this changed. Up to then we had run neck and neck. He had been the better cricketer but I had been the better mathematician. We had both done equally badly at Cambridge, but I – with a six-year break for the war – could offer the better excuse. We had both been equally indifferent soldiers, but I had at least started from the ranks; and a wound in the head was surely more glorious than trench fever. We had been companions, but now our ways were to part. Admittedly fortune had then smiled on him. He had been "not wholly the wrong person in the right place at the right time". Admittedly fortune was now frowning on me. I was the wrong person in the wrong place with qualifications nobody wanted. But this didn't alter the fact that he had pressed on to become a famous writer and here was I staring up at him, filled with resentment. Other fathers were reaching down helping hands to their sons. But what was mine doing? What, to be fair, could mine do? He had made his own way by his own efforts and he had left behind him no path that could be followed. But were they entirely his own efforts? Hadn't I come into it somewhere? In pessimistic moments, when I was trudging London in search of an employer wanting to make use of such talents as I could offer, it seemed to me, almost, that my father had got to where he was by climbing upon my infant shoulders, that he had filched from me my good name and had left me with nothing but the empty fame of being his son.

This was the worst period for me. It was a period when, suitably encouraged, my bitterness would overflow. On one or two occasions it overflowed more publicly than it should have done, so that there seemed to be only one thing to do: to escape from it all, to keep out of the limelight. Sorry, I don't give interviews. Sorry, I don't answer letters. It is better to say nothing than to say something I might regret.

That is how I saw it, looking up at him. How did he see it, looking down at me? Neither of us knew what the other thought. We could only guess. Did he guess right? Did he sympathize? Was he resentful? Did he have any feelings of guilt? Well, he had his own battles to fight and, curiously, they were not dissimilar from mine. If I was jealous of him, he was no less jealous of himself. If I wanted to escape from Christopher Robin, so, too, did he.

It is easier in England (he wrote) to make a reputation than to lose one. I wrote four 'Children's books', containing altogether, I suppose, 70,000 words – the number of words in the average-length novel. Having said good-bye to all that in 70,000 words, knowing that as far as I was concerned the mode was outmoded, I gave up writing children's books. I wanted to escape from them as I had once wanted to escape from *Punch*; as I have always wanted to escape. In vain. . . . As a discerning critic pointed out: the hero of my latest play, God help it, was "just Christopher Robin grown up". So that even when I stop writing about children I still insist on writing about people who were children once. What an obsession with me children are become![1]

He was forty-six when *The House at Pooh Corner* was published. Up to then his star had been steadily ascending: editor of *Granta*, assistant editor of *Punch*, successful playwright, and now author of four brilliant children's books. But *The House at Pooh Corner* was to mark his meridian. After that came the

[1] *It's Too Late Now.*

decline. He was writing just as fluently, just as gracefully. But fluency and grace were not enough: the public wanted stronger meat. His last play was put on in 1938: it was a failure. During the war he returned to light verse, and for a number of weeks A. A. M. was back again in *Punch*. His skill had not deserted him, but his public had; and eventually the editor, E. V. Knox, wrote to tell him so. After the war he turned to short stories. He had always written what he had wanted to write. His luck was that this was also what the public wanted to read. Now his luck was deserting him. People didn't want books of short stories. Nor did they want long philosophical poems. Nor even collections of random reflections. He at the top of the hill, I at the bottom: we each had our sorrows, our moments of disillusion. We were both of us unwanted.

Well, if nobody wanted me, if nobody was looking for a very shy young man who had once been quite good at solving differential equations, who knew how to build a Bailey Bridge and defuse a Tellermine, who had scraped a third class Honours Degree in English Literature, and who was handy with a tenon saw, if nobody would employ me, I must employ myself. I toyed with the idea of making furniture. In the end I decided to sell books.

"I would have thought," said my mother, who always hit the nail on the head no matter whose fingers were in the way, "I would have thought that this was the one thing you would have absolutely hated. I thought you didn't like 'business'. You certainly didn't get on at John Lewis. And you're going to have to meet Pooh fans all the time. Really it does seem a very odd decision." She was quite right, of course. I was no businessman. There were certainly drawbacks to the idea. However hard I tried to play down Christopher Robin, however little space I allowed on my shelves to the Pooh Books, people would inevitably think of mine as "The Christopher Robin Book-shop". However much I wanted to succeed as a bookseller on my own merits, people would inevitably conclude that I was succeeding partly at least on my father's reputation. They might even think (wrongly) that my father's money was subsidising the venture and that – unlike other less fortunate booksellers – I did not really need to make ends meet. "It's easy for him," they might say. And to some small extent this might be true, though I would do my utmost to make it as little true as possible.

On the other hand there were compensations. For here was something my wife and I could do together as partners; here was something we could do in a part of England of our own choosing; and if I wasn't too happy about four of the books, there were still plenty of others.

So in 1951 we left London for Dartmouth; and twenty-one years later we celebrated our coming of age. If, immediately after the war, fortune had frowned, from 1951 onwards it smiled. We had had the good luck to be not wholly the wrong people opening the right shop at the right time in the right town.

Of course, Christopher Robin has intruded, however hard I have tried to keep him at bay; and he still fills me with acute embarrassment.

"So this is the original. Well, well! Come over here a minute, Mandy love. Come and say how-do-you-do to Christopher Robin. Come on. Don't be shy. Shake hands with the gentleman. There now. You can tell your little friends that you've shaken hands with Christopher Robin." After years of practice I am still terribly bad at this sort of thing.

Many years ago a woman followed me into our office (if you could call it that) at the back of the shop. She leaned over my desk. "What are you writing?" she asked with a coy smile. "An invoice," I said. "Oh." Her face fell. "I thought it might have been a book."

No. Booksellers don't often write books. They know only too well that there are already far too many. Also they haven't the time. Writing a book is not the sort of thing one can do (or rather not the sort of thing I can do) in the office between serving a customer and preparing an invoice. If by any chance a bookseller does write a book, it is because he feels he must: because the urge and the opportunity combine to say "Now! This is the moment. Take your typewriter and away to the attic with you!" Ripeness – as anyone who has had to study *King Lear* for his English Tripos will tell you – is all.

The first fairy to visit the cradle had said "He shall have his father's brains and his mother's hands." When she had vanished a second fairy appeared. "And his name shall be famous throughout the world." Yes, it was another one of those cryptic spells that fairies have always been so good at, those spells that sound like a blessing but are in fact something of a curse. To be fair, in my particular case, it was again a bit of both. It is tempting, but of course quite impossible, to try and separate the blessing from the curse, to weigh them up and calculate which has been the greater. Tempting but impossible, and I shall never know whether or not I would have been better off as Charles Robert – or even Rosemary.

Some years ago I had a letter from a small child in America. She was very, very angry with me because – so she had heard – I didn't like being Christopher Robin. If she had been Christopher Robin, she told me, she would have been VERY PROUD, and I ought to be ashamed of myself for not feeling proud, too. It was a "Wol" letter, naturally: I doubt if she expected it to be otherwise. She will be older now. Older, wiser, more tolerant. And if she happens on this book she may perhaps understand just how and why it all came about.

"Pooh", said Christopher Robin earnestly, "if I – if I'm not quite –" he stopped and tried again – "Pooh, *whatever* happens, you *will* understand, won't you?"

I like to think that Pooh understood. I hope that now others will understand too.